THE CRAWFORD ARMS
"By patience I overcome difficulties"

KIOWA

A Woman Missionary in Indian Territory

ISABEL CRAWFORD

Introduction to the Bison Books Edition
by Clyde Ellis

UNIVERSITY OF NEBRASKA PRESS
LINCOLN AND LONDON

Introduction to the Bison Books Edition © 1998 by the
University of Nebraska Press
Manufactured in the United States of America

⊗ The paper in this book meets the minimum requirements
of American National Standard for Information Sciences—
Permanence of Paper for Printed Library Materials,
ANSI Z39.48-1984.

Frist Bison Books printing: 1998
Most recent printing indicated by the last digit below:
10   9   8   7   6   5   4   3   2   1

Library of Congress Cataloging-in-Publication Data
Crawford, Isabel, 1865–1961
Kiowa: a woman missionary in Indian Territory / Isabel
Crawford; introduction to the Bison Books edition by Clyde
Ellis.
p. cm.
Originally published: New York: F. H. Revell Co., c1915. With
new introd.
Includes bibliographical references.
ISBN 0-8032-6387-2 (pa: alk. paper)
1. Crawford, Isabel, 1865–1961. 2. Kiowa Indians—Mis-
sions. 3. Women missionaries—Oklahoma—Biography.
4. Baptists—Missions—Oklahoma—History. I. Title.
E99.K5C8   1998
266'.61'092—dc21
[B]
97-49932   CIP

Reprinted from the original 1915 edition, titled *Kiowa: The
History of a Blanket Indian Mission*, by the Fleming H.
Revell Company, New York. This Bison Books edition follows
the original in beginning chapter 1 on arabic page 13; no
material has been omitted.

Introduction to the Bison Books Edition

"She Gave Us The Jesus Way":
Isabel Crawford, the Kiowa People, and
the Saddle Mountain Indian Baptist Church

Clyde Ellis

At the east end of the Saddle Mountain Indian Baptist Church cemetery near Mountain View, Oklahoma, there is a modest granite grave marker bearing the inscription "I Dwell Among Mine Own People." The tombstone and its message are not out of place in this isolated cemetery, where rows of stones bear witness to the power of the Christian gospel carried by missionaries to the Kiowa-Comanche-Apache Reservation in the late nineteenth and early twentieth centuries. Numerous crosses, small American flags, piles of artificial flowers, and small bundles of tobacco laid on the graves confirm that this is sacred and powerful space, for it is here that part of the collective memory of the Kiowa people has been laid to rest during the last century.

But the marker bearing the inscription "I Dwell Among Mine Own People" does not memorialize a Kiowa; it celebrates the remarkable life of Isabel Crawford, a Canadian who arrived at the reservation in 1893 as a twenty-eight-year-old missionary. By the time of her departure in 1906, Crawford had not only overseen the creation of a flourishing church, she had endured a life-changing experience. Although she lived another fifty-five years, her work at Saddle Mountain remained the indelible moment in her life and in the lives of the Kiowa people with whom she shared thirteen extraordinary years. She never forgot them and in 1906 declared that she "would sooner lie hidden among the tall weeds of the unkept Indian cemetery . . . than in any other burial ground in the whole world." In 1961, true to her word, she came home to Saddle Mountain and the Kiowas, who have never forgotten her.[1]

Born 26 May 1865 in Cheltenham, Canada, to a Scottish father and Irish mother, Isabel Alice Hartley Crawford spent her childhood surrounded by the gospel and education. Her mother, "a perfect, good mother, a perfect lady, and a recognized scholar," wrote Crawford, dutifully oversaw her education. Her father, a Baptist minister, had emigrated to Canada from England in the early 1860s and found work in a succession of parishes and colleges in Canada and North Dakota. Surrounded by loving siblings and the excitement of frontier life, Crawford was a happy child. "While helping father in his church work, and not letting mother do any of the housework," she wrote, "I posed as an elocutionist on father's lecture tours, gave entertainments, saved my money, had a cat, a dog, a pony, and beaux overlapping one another like the prophets of old."[2]

Although she never formally graduated from high school, Crawford developed under her parents' tutelage a remarkably agile mind that she joined to a quick and biting wit. Schooled at home and also in her father's various college classrooms, Crawford remembered "six happy years" as a teenager when "night-after-night, in our simple home, full of books, mother instructed me in the best literature of the ages. . . . At nine o'clock, father came from the study and bible topics were discussed till bedtime." Admittedly a difficult student, Crawford recalled that she "learned enough history to know that my relations were all well educated and prided themselves on their 'blue blood'; enough geography to be in unknown quarters when there was a . . . French lesson on the breeze; enough arithmetic to calculate my distance when I was forbidden to be on the street and caught sight of my mother turning the corner; enough grammar to puzzle strangers who couldn't reconcile such good English with such bad behavior; enough music to alarm every living creature within range of the sound; and enough physiology to know that I was as sound as any one."[3]

Above all, Crawford's parents instilled in her a devotion to the church that decisively shaped her life. "Father felt called to preach the gospel above everything else on earth," Crawford once wrote; the enthusiasm spilled over at home, where the family worshiped twice a day and paid close attention to the dictates of conscience and scripture. Baptized at age ten ("I did want to be a Christian," she wrote, "even if I wasn't anxious about my soul. I knew I was a terror, but I longed in my heart to be a holy terror"), she was teaching Sunday School by age eleven with "the toughest urchins ever" and "taking up theology and putting down theologues" as a teenager. "I was . . . always hoping to be a missionary when I grew up," she remembered. "I didn't know then what I know now, that it is easier for God to make the giggle of a girl praise him than 'the wrath of man.'"[4]

At the age of eighteen, however, during her father's stint at Prairie College in Rapid City, Manitoba, a turning point occurred when Crawford collapsed after an especially grueling two weeks spent working in the grain fields. Stricken with consumption, she spent the next six months in bed. Her doctor (of the "kind-hearted Baptist" variety who refused to charge for his services) administered milk and quinine in generous quantities. "The quinine took possession of my ears," wrote Crawford; "the milk saved my life. But from that time until now my hearing has been bad." In fact, her illness had monumental consequences. Instead of leaving Crawford's hearing merely "bad," the fever left her almost completely deaf. For the rest of her life she relied on hearing aids and lip reading. Moreover, the lingering consequences of consumption plagued her for the rest of her life. Though spared the life of an invalid, she once confided, her health was never robust and she admitted herself on at least one occasion to a sanitarium.[5]

In Crawford's opinion, however, the ordeal was a providential sign. "At one time the household was called in to see me breathe my last," she later wrote, "but instead of 'kicking the bucket' . . . eighty-four pounds of me got up, and in three years I had quite recovered. I can now see that during all this time the Lord had been giving me such an education for future usefulness as I could not have gotten in any school in the land."[6] For by now, she began to believe that God had tested, and then spared, her for important work.

She spoke with increasing conviction about mission work and in 1886, at the age of twenty, wrote an impassioned letter to the Women's American Baptist Home Mission Society. "For some years back," she began, "the spirit of God has been working with me and has shown me so distinctly that I am one of those called to 'Go into all the world,' that at last I have yieldeth body, soul, and spirit and now find myself waiting for the fire." As if to dispel doubts about the seriousness of a twenty-year-old, Crawford wrote that she felt herself directed "so clearly to the mission work that I feel I must enter it or else live the rest of my life condemned before God. . . . I long, *Oh how I long* to be in a position where I can think about Jesus all the time. . . . I want to be a missionary of the cross; I want to obey my master's mandate '*Go*' and I want to live that humble christlike life that none can help but admire. I ask you to pray, oh do pray for me that the '*plain path*' may be pointed out to me."[7]

By 1891 Crawford had decided that the plain path led for the time being to Chicago and the Baptist Missionary Training School. On her application Crawford stated that she was "slightly deaf," "perfectly healthy," and not interested in obtaining a doctor of divinity certificate ("I have a peculiar dislike to the fraternity"). An administrator observed that she was "unsettled in her mind about going into full-time Christian work" but quite certain about her calling to mission work. "My heavenly father is leading me not by the still waters but by the troubled seas," she wrote, "but I do so long to follow where he leads." In a letter of recommendation, G. W. Huntley, a Baptist missionary and family friend, wrote that Crawford was "fairly well educated and has expressed to me the desire for Foreign Mission Work. . . . She has qualifications to make a good Home Missionary," he continued, "is bright, energetic, and ambitious to do good. If she remains single by all means receive her."[8] She remained single (apparently by breaking her engagement to Reverend W. A. Waldo, a Baptist minister), the school accepted her, and in 1893 Crawford graduated after completing the two-year course of study.

What to do and where to go? Crawford thought she knew. In her 1886 epistle to Mary Burdette, Crawford had mentioned that during a recent visit to Toronto she had "spent much time among the poor & wretched, and the success with which I met makes me think that I am more especially fitted to go about some big city and search out the poor, the blind, the halt, etc. I can serve the master anywhere," she concluded, "but I should like to decide where as soon as possible."[9]

When the word came that the Women's Baptist Home Mission Society had assigned her to the Kiowa-Comanche-Apache Reservation in southwestern Oklahoma ("87 miles from the railroad!" she lamented), Crawford was crestfallen. Calling the assignment a "complete surprise and a shock," she later recalled that she "had never been one bit interested in the Indians at any time in my life. I had seen a few in Manitoba, but they never appealed to me. For two weeks I was in a state of perfect rebellion." As the shock wore off, Crawford reconciled herself to the decision and wrote Burdette: "I have got more than I asked, but I'll go to the Indians if I am scalped twenty-four hours after I land." Crawford arrived at Elk Creek on the Kiowa-Comanche Agency 23 November 1893.[10]

The Kiowa-Comanche-Apache Reservation was one of the most important in the entire country. Created by the 1867 Medicine Lodge Treaty, its three and a half million acres in the southwest corner of Oklahoma Territory were home to more than six thousand Indians from ten tribes. The Bureau of Indian Affairs considered this reservaton one of the most critical tests of the government's post–Civil War "civilizing" policy, and observers scrutinized it. Here, under the watchful gaze of teachers, missionaries, and government farmers, policymakers hoped that the tribes would build a future in which they would be culturally indistinguishable from their white patrons—civilized, industrious, Christianized, white in every way except skin color.[11]

At the center of government policy lay two closely related enterprises—schools and churches. Together, reformers said, they would lead the tribes up from savagery and into civilization. In 1898, for example, Commissioner of Indian Affairs William A. Jones stated with absolute conviction that "education is the greatest factor in solving the future status of the Indian." Religious leaders echoed the belief. "Do you not see that Christianity will civilize them?" wrote Mary Burdette. "When they become Christians they 'cut off,' as they express it, the old superstitions." Though Agent Lawrie Tatum described the Kiowas and Comanches as "probably the worst Indians east of the Rocky Mountains," he put his faith in the power of Quaker goodness. "My fervent desire was to be supplied with heavenly wisdom sufficient for the responsible business devolving upon me," he wrote. "My trust was in the Lord, who could restrain the evil intentions and passions of the Indians." The pioneering Indian educator Richard Pratt put the matter in terms that Crawford could appreciate. When it came to Indians, he wrote, "I am a Baptist because I believe in immersing the Indians in our civilization and when we get them under holding them until they are thoroughly soaked."[12]

Already well established in the eastern half of the territory, the Baptists arrived in force at the Kiowa-Comanche Agency in the late 1880s and by the early 1890s established a handful of missions. Deeply moved by the urgency of the work ("The Blanket Indians of Oklahoma are begging for help," went one plea; "I know of no place where one can be so . . . practically useful in the world, and where orthodox denominational views are no barrier," went another), the Women's Baptist Home Mission Society sent Isabel Crawford and Hattie Everts to join fellow missionaries Marietta Reeside and Laura Ballew. Baptist ministers George W. Hicks, Howard H. Clouse, and E. C. Deyo also were there. Between them they opened Elk Creek and Rainy Mountain Missions in 1893 and 1894 among the Kiowas and the Deyo Mission among the Comanches in 1894.[13]

Although warned that "mission work means privation," Crawford later remembered that conditions at Elk Creek were so crude that they made "my blood run cold." "Have not been able to have a good bath for three weeks till to-day," she reported shortly after arriving. "I've been washing one foot (twelve inches) at a time," she continued, "but to-day I got two cups of rain water and had a good bath." Difficult conditions notwithstanding, Crawford reveled at the chance to do so much. "Am in excellent health and cheerful as a cricket," she wrote in 1894. "Don't worry one bit or 'write me every week,' for I wouldn't leave Elk Creek for anything, and some day all this rough work will be done. . . . Please don't think I'm having too many hardships. I can stand more yet. He never sends too many. I'll stand anything if I can see even one soul saved."[14]

Despite her determination to stay on until the work was done, Crawford's health faltered and she suffered a crisis of confidence. By 1894 she had come to hope that the Board of Home Missions would not keep her in the Indian Territory. "I hoped in my very soul that I would not be asked to set foot in the Territory," Crawford later remembered, "but the Lord sent me back, and I worked like a galley slave." By early 1896 Crawford expressed relief that the Lord was leading her away from Elk Creek; she was not, however, leaving the Kiowas. Instead, Crawford moved thirty miles east in April 1896 to Saddle Mountain, whose more than three hundred Kiowas had no mission. "Lone Wolf and Big Tree [prominent Kiowa chiefs near Rainy Mountain] got the churches," said one Saddle Mountain Kiowa, "but the Indians live over here."[15]

Despite having to live in a tent under grueling conditions, Crawford was optimistic about her new post. One year after arriving she had satisfied herself that "the Lord led me away from Elk Creek to a point as good if not better than any point yet taken by the Baptists here." Two years after arriving she was "satisfied that these years have been ordered of the Lord." Moreover, she felt needed at Saddle Mountain in a way she hadn't at Elk Creek. "Up to this year [1898] I have only been able to hold onto the work; now the Lord, I think, is putting us in a position to push a little," she observed. "The Indians are progressing nicely—more, perhaps, spiritually than physically, for they make more of an effort 'to catch the Jesus road' than to catch a plow. They never had such opportunities to succeed." Encouraged by the work, in May 1898 she and the Kiowas formed a local mission society and named it "Daw-kee-boom-gee-k'oop," Kiowa for "God's Light on the Mountain."[16]

Yet here, as at Elk Creek, Crawford endured conditions that brought her again to the edge of collapse. Her health began to deteriorate while she lived first in a tent and then in a lean-to. "I confess now for the first time that the work is too much for one," she wrote in 1897, "and I am not able to do more than half that should be done. This winter I have not enjoyed my usual health and had it not been for the long hard ride to the RR I should probably have gone home." Unwilling to abandon the Kiowas, however, she proposed a solution: send another missionary to assist her. But not just any missionary. "No *young* woman is willing to do this, no matter how much she may honestly think so. . . . Not one woman in a thousand is able to stand it *in such a way as to teach Christ*." The one woman Crawford believed could bear the strain was Mary McLean, a friend from Canada and a fellow graduate of the Baptist Missionary Training School. McLean informed Crawford that she could not "do the missionary part of the work, but I'm sure I can take some of the responsibilities off your shoulders." When she arrived at Saddle Mountain in early October 1897, Crawford sensed the beginning of a new era. Five years later, on 9 November 1902, the cornerstone for the church building was laid.[17]

In addition to McLean, Reeside, and Ballew, Crawford also enlisted the aid of Lucius Aitsan, one of the most remarkable Kiowas in the Saddle Mountain community. Crawford would later write that it was largely due to his efforts as interpreter and assistant that the work went forward as smoothly as it did. Educated for three years at Carlisle Indian School, Aitsan could read and write English and was a devout Christian and a stalwart at the mission from the very beginning. He had interpreted for other missions, including the Catholic priests (who spoke so quickly, he said, that he could not keep up with them and asked finally to be excused) and the Baptists, who baptized him at Elk Creek in June 1896. Quietly encouraged by the sermons he heard, Aitsan later recalled that "I hid all their wise talks in my heart" and discovered that "there was a man just like me in the Bible. He believed the best way he knew how, and Jesus knew it." Anxious to see the Saddle Mountain Kiowas get their own mission, he "never told anybody, but I asked Jesus on the sly to send a Jesus woman to our district and to my home that I might learn more."[18]

Devoted to Crawford and the work at Saddle Mountain, Aitsan worked tirelessly. He visited the camps to introduce her, convinced skeptical Kiowas to listen to her message, and along with his wife, Mabel, looked after Crawford's daily needs. He also came to her assistance in other matters. When Crawford wrote to Mary Burdette on 13 May 1897 to request the services of Mary McLean, for example, Aitsan did the same. "I would like to write a few words to you and to let you know what I want you to do for us at the Saddle Mountain Kiowas," he began. "I wants [sic] you to send another missionary over here," he continued, because the work was "too much work for her, so we thought we would like to have other lady with Miss Crawford." Besides, he added, "at Rainy Mountain Mission they are three of them [missionaries] and . . . very few Kiowas on Rainy Mountain Creek and those missionary workers they do not do very much." In time, Aitsan became one of the most influential Kiowa Christians on the reservation. Ordained as a minister on 13 June 1913, he died in the influenza epidemic of 1918, leaving the Saddle Mountain community grief-stricken. "His abrupt passing in 1918," wrote Harlan Hall, "made many tribesmen wonder at what might have been."[19]

From the ten years Crawford spent at Saddle Mountain came *Kiowa*, originally published in 1915. Written "to contradict the statement that 'the only good Indian is a dead one,'" it was derived from the journals she kept faithfully during her life, edited and condensed "to leave out all that was hardest and most disagreeable."[20] Sprightly written, self-effacing, Crawford's narrative is a remarkable work, still valuable nearly a century later. Chief among the reasons is its unique perspective. A young, single woman, Crawford gives us a kind of insight rarely found in the literature on the Kiowa-Comanche Agency. As a "Jesus Woman," the Kiowas thought of her as a special envoy—brave but demure, strong but dependent on their good will. "No White Jesus man ever sat down with us," one Kiowa told Crawford shortly after her arrival. "You, one white woman, all alone among

Indians and no scared—this is good." As a result, their mutual relationships tended to be subtly different from those with male missionaries and ministers. Some Indians regarded some male missionaries and ministers as authority figures to be obeyed and sometimes feared ("White men are dangerous," said one Kiowa man); Kiowas accepted Crawford as a member of the community: "She was the first one to live among the Indians," remembered Tonemah, a Saddle Mountain deacon, in 1928. "She was just like a mother, she taught us the way to Christ. All these years she has not forgotten us. We want to say that we want her back."[21]

And although she was a dedicated missionary whose greatest dream was to bring Kiowa people into the church, Crawford's commentary is refreshingly free of the narrow-minded if well-intentioned rhetoric typical of missionaries. She was relieved that the Kiowas appeared to be relinquishing what she and others casually referred to as "savage habits," and she never tired of extolling work, thrift, and Christian love—virtues she insisted were contradictory to Kiowa values. Yet Crawford also insisted that missionaries do more than simply order Indians to work or denigrate them for their failures. "Now it is time to roll up our sleeves to show them how," she wrote. "I wonder how many of us would be working to-day if our parents or guardians had said 'Let them alone; let us see what they will do.'" "Pray for the Indians," she lamented, for "we have ruined them." Willing to share the middle ground, she expressed a level of cultural sensitivity rare for the era. "We are not here *to boss* the Indians," she wrote in 1898, "but to do what they let us when it is not wrong. If they are not 'citizens' on earth they are citizens of heaven and no person has a right to domineer over them."[22]

Finally, Crawford and her memoir matter because of their place in the Kiowa community today. What she and the Saddle Mountain Kiowas did has become an integral

part of Kiowa history that continues to be told and retold
as part of a community-wide narrative. Unlike many
academically positioned narratives that attack
missionaries as ill-informed and malicious, Crawford's
memoir, and the powerful accounts offered by Kiowas,
suggest a more complicated encounter. For their part, the
Kiowas recognized that accepting Christianity need not
come at the cost of their larger cultural identity, but did
much to shape the contours of twentieth-century Kiowa
life. "Church, dining hall, Tabernacle, parsonage, sheds
for her buggy, barn for her pony, and baptistery," wrote
Tully Morrison, "each has a story, they were built with
the Indians' help." Moreover, these stories are not about
the collapse of Kiowa culture, they are about its ability to
endure change and to accommodate new ideas. Mary
Aitson, who married one of Lucius's grandsons, said, "We
always remember her when we go down there on
Memorial Day to clean the graves. She always seemed
like a member of our family." At the same time, she noted,
"I married into the Aitson family 44 years ago, and I'm
always amazed at how they stay with their traditions."[23]

In letters and diaries of their own, Kiowa people
expressed their Christian devotion even as they continued
to maintain Kiowa identity. In these narratives,
missionaries are not the enemy and Christianity is not
evil. "I feel like you do about the Kiowas," wrote Gotebo, a
Kiowa leader, to Reverend J. S. Murrow in 1897. "I am
hungry to see them all come into the Jesus road and be
saved. Oh how good is Jesus' road. . . . I wish that every
tribe of Indians would follow Jesus." Another Kiowa man,
Goomda, recalled in 1934 "how the Word was shot into
my heart when I first heard the Gospel." John Queton,
whose mother was one of the first seven Kiowas baptized
at Elk Creek, wrote in 1943 "to thank the American Baptist
Home Missionary Society for all the splendid help they
have given my race."[24]

Kiowa ends in 1906 but does not reveal the circumstances of Crawford's departure. She left Saddle Mountain in December 1906 as the result of a bitter doctrinal dispute that pitted her against the ministers and her own Mission Board. By 1905 Crawford had become impatient with the local ministers, whose willingness to serve communion and handle other official duties was at best uneven. Consequently, she encouraged the congregation to decide for itself if its own deacons should assume responsibility for serving communion. The members voted in favor, and shortly thereafter Lucius Aitsan served communion. Outraged, local Baptist ministers publicly criticized Crawford, rebuked her personally, and wrote a series of stormy letters that eventually produced an official reprimand against the Saddle Mountain Church and a campaign for her ouster.

Stunned by the episode but unwilling to expose the congregation to what promised to be an ugly confrontation, Crawford announced in December 1906 her plans to accept a post in New York. The congregation, bewildered by the turn of events, implored her to stay, but the dispute had fatally compromised her position. "You could hardly recede from the stand you have taken without injuring your influence," wrote Charles Stanton. "The Indians would say, 'If Miss Crawford is mistaken about this road, she may be about others also.' Their confidence in you would be shaken. You can retire as it is, true to your principles and strong in the feeling that you are right."[25] Crawford left but remained scarred from the episode.

Exiled from the Kiowas, Crawford spent the next two decades working for the Mission Board in a series of other positions. But she yearned to return to the Kiowas and in 1927 began making inquiries about retiring to Saddle Mountain to live out her life as an assistant at the church. The Kiowas and their current missionary, Perry Jackson, enthusiastically endorsed the idea, but Crawford had by that time managed to alienate almost everyone in a position to help her. As early as 1908, H. L. Morehouse,

the corresponding secretary of the American Baptist Home
Mission Society, informed a friend that Crawford's letters
concerning the 1905 episode contained "a very vindictive
spirit. . . . She made herself so offensive," he continued,
"that I cannot have any relations with her." Appalled by
Crawford's crassness, Mrs. John Nuveen wondered how
it was possible "for Miss Crawford to lose her womanliness
as to write such an impertinent letter." Uncharacter-
istically contrite, Crawford apologetically informed
Morehouse that "I need not tell you what brought me to
this nerve-wracked condition for *you know and I know
and God knows*." "An attack of nervous prostration after
the tragedy at Saddle Mountain," she revealed, had left
her "crushed into a cripple for weary months and years to
come." In desperation, she had found it necessary to enter
a sanitarium.[26]

Still seething two decades later, she wrote angrily of
"the final crash, when no one could save me, and I was
crushed in the denominational machinery and God's plan
for my life completely wrecked!" In 1929 she wrote a friend
that "one would think instead of my hard yet successful
work to spread the gospel, I had been guilty of murder in
the first degree. But since I was a woman, life
imprisonment was substituted for the electric chair. The
polite thing for me to do I suppose is to step in front of a
speeding auto and be killed instantly, but I refuse to satisfy
the missionary committee . . . in this way." *Kiowa* proved
to be her revenge. "I quit," she recalled, "and wrote *Kiowa*
without making a single reference to the tragedy."[27]

In September 1929, the American Baptist Home
Missionary Society and the Women's Baptist Home
Missionary Society voted unanimously that it was "unwise
for Miss Crawford to return to Saddle Mountain to make
her home there or to become a part of the staff there."
Crawford resigned six weeks later in an emotion-filled
letter that barely concealed her bitterness: "God's plan
for my life," she acidly observed, "has been wrecked *the*

second time.[28] She went quietly into retirement, returned to her native Canada, and lived with two nieces until her death on 18 November 1961, at the age of ninety-six.

By the time of Crawford's death, Saddle Mountain Indian Baptist Church was nearing the end of its days. The congregation had dwindled and the building had slipped into disrepair; a local rancher had plans to use it for hay storage. In November 1963, Herbert Westner purchased the church building after locals implored him to help save it and moved it to the nearby town of Cache, where today it sits on Westner's property. Indian congregations continue to worship in it, and the building is in good repair.[29]

The original site of the church is now pastureland, but a small trailer is home to a congregation. The Kiowas maintain the cemetery, bury their people in the shadow of Saddle Mountain, and remember the Jesus Lady from Canada whom they claimed as one of their own, naming her Geeahhoangomah—"She Gave Us The Jesus Way." Nestled in the hills of the Wichita Mountains, the cemetery is a soulful place, quiet and beautiful. Crawford is there with Lucius Aitsan. Together, at rest among their people, they watch over each other, over their legacy, and over Dawkeeboomgeek'oop.

NOTES

1. Isabel Crawford, "Among Mine Own People," *The Watchman Examiner*, 14 May 1942; Tully Morrison, "Isabel Crawford: Missionary to the Kiowa Indians," *Chronicles of Oklahoma* 40:1 (spring 1962): 77. When Crawford reminded the Saddle Mountain congregation during a 1927 Christmas visit of her wish to be buried at that place, John Onko, a member of the church, replied, "We understand that when you pass on you have arranged to bury yourself here with the Indians. We want these words put on your tomb-stone: 'I dwell among mine

own people.' " Another member of the church grumbled about the circumstances under which the beloved Crawford would return: "We don't want you to bring your died body back. We want to you to bring your live body back and stay by it." See Isabel Crawford, "My Later Trip to Bacone, Elk Creek, and Saddle Mountain," January 1928, Indian Missions: Correspondence Files for Oklahoma, American Baptist Archives, Valley Forge PA (hereafter cited as IMCF, ABA). In 1944 Coe Hayne observed that "acquaintance with her [Crawford] is not complete until one has met and conversed with the Kiowa, her beloved Indians." See W. S. McLay, "May There Be Roses In December For Her!" in Coe Hayne, *Kiowa Turning* (New York: American Baptist Home Mission Society, 1944), 48.

2. Crawford told her life story in an autobiography, *Joyful Journey: Highlights on the High Way* (Philadelphia: Judson Press, 1951). Crawford is quoted from a brief biographical sketch written by her sometime after her retirement in 1930. "Isabel Crawford," Isabel Crawford Collection, American Baptist Archives, Valley Forge PA, 2 (hereafter cited as ICC, ABA). Crawford's life is also discussed in *The Heroine of Saddle Mountain* (Chicago: Woman's American Baptist Home Mission Society, 1917), a tract based largely on her journals and published works. A fictional account of Crawford's work at Saddle Mountain appeared in 1987; see Leonard Sanders, *Light on the Mountain* (New York: Bantam, 1986).

3. "Isabel Crawford," ICC, ABA, 1; *Heroine of Saddle Mountain*, 3–4.

4. Crawford, *Joyful Journey*, 19, 54; *Heroine of Saddle Mountain*, 5; "Isabel Crawford," ICC, ABA, 2.

5. Crawford, *Joyful Journey*, 26; *Heroine of Saddle Mountain*, 6; "Isabel Crawford," ICC, ABA, 3; Crawford to H. L. Morehouse, 11 February 1908, ICC, ABA.

6. *Heroine of Saddle Mountain*, 6.

7. Crawford to Mary Burdette, 8 March 1886, ICC, ABA.

8. "From the Application of Isabelle [sic] Crawford—1891, Class of 1893 At BMTS," ICC, ABA, 1–2; G. W. Huntley to Mary Burdette, 16 July 1891, ICC, ABA.

9. Crawford to Burdette, 8 March 1886, ICC, ABA.

10. Crawford, *Joyful Journey*, 54–55; *Heroine of Saddle Mountain*, 7; "Isabel Crawford," ICC, ABA, 3–4.

11. One of the most important aspects of Crawford's memoir is that it offers a rare view into the day-to-day workings of reservation life. Other first-hand accounts include Thomas C. Battey, *The Life and Adventures of a Quaker among the Indians*, introduction by Alice Marriott (1875; reprint, Norman: University of Oklahoma Press, 1968); and Lawrie Tatum, *Our Red Brothers and the Peace Policy of President Ulysses S. Grant*, foreword by Richard Ellis (1899; reprint, Lincoln: University of Nebraska Press, 1970). The best secondary account of the era is William T. Hagan, *United States–Comanche Relations: The Reservation Years* (Norman: University of Oklahoma Press, 1990).

12. *Annual Report of the Commissioner of Indian Affairs*, 1898, 2; Mary Burdette, ed., *Young Women among Blanket Indians: The Trio At Rainy Mountain* (Chicago: R. R. Donnelley and Sons, 1898), 27; Tatum, *Our Red Brothers*, 25, 35; Richard Pratt, *Battlefield and Classroom: Four Decades with the American Indian, 1867–1904*, edited and with an introduction by Robert M. Utley (New Haven: Yale University Press, 1964) 335.

13. "The Kiowa Indians, Early Beginnings of Baptist Missionary Work,"IMCF, ABA; Burdette, *Young Women among the Blanket Indians*, 7, 11; Robert Hamilton, *The Gospel among the Red Men* (Nashville: Sunday School Board of the Southern Baptist Convention, 1930), 203–7; Hugh D. Corwin, "Protestant Mission Work among the Comanches and Kiowas," *Chronicles of Oklahoma* 46 (spring 1968): 41–57. Corwin states that "the work of the American Baptist missionaries seems to have begun when Lone Wolf welcomed to his camp a devoted Lay preacher and carpenter, W. D. Lancaster. . . . This was in 1889" (49). For an account of Baptist work with the Kiowas, see Hayne, *Kiowa Turning*.

14. *Heroine of Saddle Mountain*, 9–11.

15. Crawford to Mary Burdette, 13 May 1897, ICC, ABA.

16. Crawford to Burdette, 13 May 1897, ICC, ABA; *Heroine of Saddle Mountain*, 27–28.

17. Crawford to Burdette, 13 May 1897, ICC, ABA.

18. See "The Interpreter's Story By Lucius Aitsan," in *Heroine of Saddle Mountain*, 19–24, and in Crawford, *Kiowa*, 33–41.

19. Lucius Aitsan to Mary Burdette, 13 May 1897, ICC, ABA; Harlan Hall to the author, 4 August 1997.

20. Crawford, *Kiowa*, xxix.

21. *Heroine of Saddle Mountain*, 18; the same story is told in Crawford, *Kiowa*, 17, 25; Tonemah quoted in "Talks By Members," delivered during Crawford's 1928 visit, IMCF, ABA, 1.

22. *Heroine of Saddle Mountain*, 11; Crawford to unknown, 4 October 1898, ICC, ABA.

23. Morrison, "Isabel Crawford," 78; Mary Aitson to the author, 22 July 1997; Mary Aitson to the author, 14 August 1997.

24. Gotebo to J. S. Murrow, 6 January 1897, IMCF, ABA; Goomda quoted in "Report on Rainy Mountain Mission," 14 April 1934, IMCF, ABA; John Queton testimony, 1943, IMCF, ABA.

25. Eleanor Hull, *Women Who Carried the Good News* (Valley Forge: Judson Press, 1975), 24.

26. H. L. Morehouse to Mrs. John Nuveen, 18 January 1908, ICC, ABA; Mrs. John Nuveen to Morehouse, 18 January 1908, ICC, ABA; Crawford to Morehouse, 11 February 1908, ICC, ABA.

27. Crawford to Katherine Westfall, 23 June 1927, IMCF, ABA; Crawford to Clara Northcutt, 24 October 1929, IMCF, ABA.

28. Frank Smith to Katherine Westfall, 19 September 1929, ICC, ABA; Crawford's letter of resignation, 2 November 1929, ICC, ABA.

29. Herbert Westner, conversation with the author, 26 July 1997.

Contents

CONTENTS

List of Illustrations

Introduction

I KNOW of no one better qualified by temperament, acquaintance, and appreciation to write concerning any phase of mission work among the American Indians (the work that during her entire mature years engaged my sister's every faculty) than Miss Isabel Crawford. I am more than glad to commend to the heart and brain of every one interested in missions among a poor, misused, and almost friendless people, the book upon her experiences and observations in Indian missionary service, which she presents to the public. It is sure to be earnest, intelligent and above all lovingly sympathetic. The children of tepee and ranch and range are happy at least in their chronicler. She has lived and wrought and thought amid the shadows, and God's sunshine has tempered these shadows with tints as tender as the changing iris on the breast of the dove, the soft grays that beautify the under-leaf of the olive, and the joy of service, the happiness of duty sings between the lines of her chronicles.

The relations between the author and my sister Mary were always mutually affectionate, and intelligently appreciative. They were loving yoke-fellows, complementing each other's qualities, each supplementing the other's strength with her own tactful collaboration. Between the missionary and the secretary there was a bond of sisterly love that was never weakened by time or circumstance. I am most cordial, then, in my commendation of "Belle Crawford's" book, and my highest hope for it is that it will be as widely read and as affectionately appreciated as her name is pleasantly known, far and wide amid the multitudes in our churches throughout the country.

ROBERT J. BURDETTE.

"Sunny Crest,"
Pasadena, California.

Preface

THIS simple story of ten years, eight months and three days of the best part of my life was written at random during exhaustive activities in tent, tepee and lodge and condensed later to leave out all that was hardest and most disagreeable.

I am indebted to Miss Harriet C. Rychen of Wyoming, Ohio, and Mrs. Phebe Sawyer of Spokane, Wash., for favors received during the writing periods, to my brother for valuable assistance rendered through the building operations and to the constituency of the Women's American Baptist Home Mission Society, without whose loyal and *spiritual* support the work at Saddle Mountain could never have been undertaken.

Splendid helpers, a cast-iron constitution, Scotch determination, Irish nonsense, the Divine call and the power of the Holy Spirit, are the elements that made for success. Had any one of them been lacking the results could not have been the same.

The aim of the book is to contradict the statement that "the only good Indian is a dead one."

It is thoughtfully dedicated to the memory of Miss Mary G. Burdette, the first person I ever heard emphasize the fact that *God called women* as well as men, not to go into all the world and *preach* the Gospel, but to go into all the world and *teach it in a simple womanly way.*

I

Beginnings—Story-Telling—Ghost Dance—
Pigs—Lucius and Mabel

" Guide me, O Thou great Jehovah,
　　Pilgrim through this barren land ;
　I am weak, but Thou art mighty,
　　Hold me with Thy powerful hand :
　　　Bread of Heaven,
　Feed me till I want no more."

APRIL 9, 1896. We were singing it with
might and main, lying on our backs on
the top of the load, when suddenly the
wagon stopped and Zotom, the Indian driver,
alighted and unhitched the unequally-yoked together horse and mule.

A new white canvas tepee apart from the rest,
facing the road over which we came instead of
the east, bade us silent welcome.

As if by magic dogs sprang from the ground
everywhere barking an alarm that brought from
tepee and tent Indian men, women and children, decked in their brightest and best.

Shading their eyes they looked up—backed
off a bit—and looked again. There we sat,
" Stand - in - the - middle - of - the - road " (Zotom's
wife) and I, on a bed tick, on the summit of a

high rickety road, "chuckling" with the hens in a coop that shared our exalted position.

Making sure they were not seeing visions they signed :

"Is it true that the leetle Jesus woman from Elk Creek has come ? "

"It is true," signed Zotom and Stand-in-the-middle-of-the-road together.

"Tell her I am so glad I can't say it," said Little Robe, and turning led the triumphant procession up from the creek towards one of the two small houses in the vicinity. Great preparations had been made.

The walls were hung with bunches of beaded eagle feathers, buckskin dresses, bows, arrows, guns and revolvers, while the bed was covered with a blanket rivaling in brilliancy Joseph's coat of many colors.

In the other room close to the walls, tepee-fashion, were stacked saddles, saddle-blankets, bridles, harnesses, biscuit-boxes, pails, tin cans, "feed" and innumerable flour sacks stuffed full of things.

Quilts and blankets were quickly brought, folded and placed upon the floor in front of these lines of goods, and then I was escorted with great decorum to the best seat, the rest taking their places on either side.

A long piece of old tepee canvas was next pulled in from outside and spread for a table-cloth (or floor cloth), cups and plates were passed, and a large handful of knives, forks and spoons were deposited at my place.

A coffee-pot and a big tin pail containing raw beef completed the preliminaries and the " Five o'clock tea" was ready.

A dead pause followed. Little Robe pointing to me said : " You, you go ahead," and every head was bowed.

Did I ask a blessing or did I return thanks?

I do not know, but I do know that the words, " Feed me till I want no more," kept ringing through my unmissionary head that night till sleep closed my weary eyes.

April 11th. How it rained as mounted on the load again we went dashing, splashing, swaying down into Sugar Creek.

Cowboys with a thousand cattle were on ahead and an Indian was off in hot pursuit with a " white man's talking paper," demanding a beef for the grass eaten.

Beef! Beef! Beef! and from every direction poured Indians on horseback with guns, followed by women and children in wagons, with axes and knives. A skinny old cow was turned over, the aim taken, the trigger pulled.

Suddenly a wagon dashed up out of the creek and there was a change in the order of business.

Red Eagle, wheeling his pony, dismounted. Reaching up the side of the load with one hand and holding his cocked gun at arm's length, with the other he shook hands so vigorously that I nearly came down head first.

"You all alone and no skeered?" he signed. "Maybe so we scalp you!"

The rest, in and out through the timber, stood solemnly erect, with hands clapped over their mouths (the sign for great surprise).

Only the cow with drooping head and panting sides remained unmoved.

A few minutes later there was a loud report and her miseries were over. Women in bare feet chopped and cut up the beef, a long warm dripping piece was placed beside us on the load and after farewells that left our hands dyed with gore, we started on our rainy way.

Saddle Mountain Creek is a little winding stream that gets its source not from one, but from many soft-water springs that rise in the foot-hills of the Wichita Mountains.

Mount Scott, Mount Sheridan, and Saddle Mountain (not yet on the map) are the three highest peaks, the latter receiving its name because of its similarity in outline to that of a Mexican saddle.

It was on Saddle Mountain Creek, soaked to the skin, that we pitched our tent, with a camp of Indians that owned three pigs.

April 12th, Sunday. It rained all night and all day.

Fortunately there was a little two-roomed house on the hill and men, women, children, dogs and missionary all crowded into it.

A roaring fire was made in the cook-stove and steam rose and fell like wreaths of smoke from an engine.

À few who had heard the news came in haste through the storm, and squeezing themselves into the mass of living, moving, damp humanity stood before me with hands raised to their mouths.

When they had recovered sufficiently from their surprise these were some of the things they signed:

" We like this. You, one woman all alone among Indians and no skeered."

" No White Jesus man ever sat down with us. One Jesus woman all alone and no skeered. This is good."

"We like you for coming this way. You trust us."

" We have no one to tell us about Jesus over here. The Great Father has brought you to us."

" We thank you for coming, but the thank you to Jesus is away ahead."

All day long a simple service continued and when darkness closed in I was glad to drop to sleep on any kind of a bed, in any kind of a corner.

April 13th.   Rain! Rain! Rain! Rain!

April 14th. Yesterday and to-day brought many Indians in on horseback to see if the report was really true that a white woman was all alone among them.

A heavy wagon drawn by spotted horses, and followed by three yellow dogs and a big black one stopped at the camp.

After the woman had wrapped the baby closer to her and made the other little girl's position safe, the man handed her the lines and dismounted.

Taking my hand and shaking it vigorously he said in good plain English :

" I am very glad you have come.   Our horses are poor and we cannot go seventeen miles to Rainy Mountain to church.   Many Indians live over here.   We want you to stay with us and we will help you all we can."

At night in a tepee round a blazing fire of logs, after the " Jesus talk," this story was told, mostly in the sign language :

" A long time ago there was an old woman who had no husband and lived all alone in a tepee, at the foot of a high rock.   The buffalo used to fall over this rock, breaking their legs, so she had plenty to eat.   One night a lot of Pawnee Indians came and told her to hurry up and get them something to eat.   She read their minds and knew they wanted to kill her. Fastening the light on her head she went out to look for the meat, and coming back put a large piece of thin fat over the coals to cook. When it was 'jumping hot' she threw it in their faces and ran.

After they had wiped the hot grease from their burned skins, they tried to catch her by following the light on her head. Hearing them coming she took the light off, put it on the edge of the rock and as they came near, threw it straight out as far as she could throw it.

They were running very fast and all fell over the rock and were killed.

This woman was a chief. You are the same. All alone and no skeered ! ''

April 16th. While out fishing to-day, Stand-in-the-middle-of-the-road ate the bait and at night told this story :

"A long time ago, when I was a little girl, my father went with a raiding party into Texas. They broke into a house one night, killed the white man, stole the woman and drove off all the stock. They tied the woman on a horse behind one of the men, but she screamed and slipped from side to side so that they stopped, after riding a long time, to hold a council about what to do with her.

They killed her and ate her with bacon ! ''

"She fool you," interrupted Zotom. "They made medicine."

"They cut out her heart, chopped it into little pieces and everybody swallowed one piece, without chewing it. They thought it would make them powerful like the white people."

It wasn't easy to give a fitting gospel-talk after this recital but we gave one without a fit and then went to bed.

April 23d. A "crazy white man" came to the camp late this afternoon and Zotom invited him into the tepee after supper to hear the "Jesus talk." Three Indians sat with loaded guns across their knees.

At the close Zotom turned to him and said :

"How is it that you are so bad when you can read the Bible for yourself? The Great Father is ashamed of you. If you had acted right we would have given you food and let you stay all night, but your heart is bad, and you must go away. It is eighteen miles to the white settlement and as you go ask the Great Father to forgive you." He rode off, a black sinner, into God's beautiful moonlight.

The lesson had been on life as a conflict with heaven as its goal and after the excitement died down this story was told :

"A long time ago a man, his wife and two children, a boy and a girl, lived in a tepee near a mountain. There were other Indians camping near. Soon the deer and buffalo were all gone and everybody was 'chuck-away-hungry.'

This man and his family moved off by themselves, and for a while found plenty of 'chuck,' but soon there was nothing to shoot and they were all hungry again.

One day the man said to his wife: 'We must both go out to hunt to-day or the children will die; you go one way and I will go the other.'

Watching till she reached the river, he picked up his gun, aimed and fired.

Then he made a fire, cut the head off the body (throwing it over into the bushes), roasted some of the nicest pieces of the flesh, called the children to eat, saying he had killed a deer, and taking his gun hurried away. The children saw the smoke, found the meat and ate heartily.

All at once they heard a strange gurgling sound from behind the bushes and their mother's voice calling, 'Children! Children! What is the matter? Don't you know you have been eating your mother? Now I'm mad and I'm going to kill you.' The children were afraid and ran and ran, but when they looked back they saw their mother's head rolling after them. The faster they ran the faster the head rolled and they didn't know what to do. They kept on running as fast as they could and after a while they met a buffalo who asked them what was the matter.

When they had told him he took something
out of his inside and gave it to them saying:
'Whenever the head gets too near throw this
at it.'

The children ran on and when the head was
nearly up to them, they threw what the buffalo
had given them at it.

A whole forest sprang from the ground, so
that the head couldn't get through for a long
time and the children got away ahead.

Then they came to a narrow deep stream on
the other side of which sat an old old Indian man
making a bow.

They called and told him their trouble. He
put the bow across the water and they walked
over on it safely.

Then the head came rolling up and said:
'Old man, I am looking for my children. Will
you help me over?'

When it had rolled half-way across, the old
man gave the bow a quick jerk, and it sank into
the water with a gurgling sound.

The children kept on running and after a
while came to a tepee and went in. Their father
was there with staring eyes. He scolded them
for eating their mother and took them out and
tied them to two trees. Then they knew that he
was crazy. Their old dog with no teeth, that
had followed their father, saw them and came
and chewed the rope that tied the boy to the

tree. As soon as he was free, he let his sister loose, and, followed by the dog, they ran and ran and ran.

Then they stopped and prayed, 'Oh, Great Spirit, save us!'

After walking a long long way they came to a beautiful tepee, on the bank of a river. Strips of buffalo meat hung under an arbor, and inside they found plenty of the nicest parts cooked and ready.

They had had a hard time but they were saved at last and their hearts laughed."

"This is a leetle the same as the Jesus-story you have been telling us," signed the narrator.

April 26th, Sunday. The sun shone, dogs barked, pigs grunted, birds sang and all nature seemed out for a frolic. The rain was past.

Two wagon sheets were tied on the top of six poles and at about eleven by the sun the service began.

Bleached bones lay about in every direction, and here and there the white skeleton head of an ancient cow loomed up, staring, staring, staring with great eyeless sockets.

A white woman had called a council and twenty-five responded.

With needle and thread in hand, I slowly picked up pieces of dead leaves, weeds, chips, etc., strung them and laid them on my lap.

"Enter ye in at the straight gate" was the subject. "You can't do this alone. God's Holy Spirit, who guided me in my heart to come to you, must guide you. If you pass through this gate into the new life your old religions, your dances, your cards, your mescal, etc., must all drop off and you will begin a spiritual fight that will last as long as you live."

As the thread was drawn through the needle and the accumulation of dead fragments fell to the ground, every face indicated that the message had been understood.

"Are there any Christians here?"

Not a hand went up but every head went down.

"Are there any who would like to give up the old roads and let the Holy Spirit teach the new?"

Two men put up their hands at once.

The younger spoke:

"I am sorry there are no Christians over here. Sometimes we all sit around to eat but there is nobody to thank Jesus, so we wait a while and think. Some Indians say when they are baptized that they bury all their bad roads and then they pick them up again and go off with them. I don't want to be that kind. I want to be a white-man Christian."

He was a man of about thirty years of age, short, stout, dark, with coal black hair and eyes, white teeth and straight legs. His wife, two children, three yellow dogs and a big black one were with him.

White people called him Lucius but the Indians clung to the old name "Aitsan," which means, "Killed-him-on-the-sly."

In the afternoon in the bottom of a wagon we drove seven miles to Sugar Creek, where a number of Indians, in holiday attire, sat under an arbor made of branches of trees. We talked to them about Jesus and at the close four men, wrapped from their heads to their feet in white sheets, emerged from a big white tepee close to the arbor. One behind the other they came towards me and in turn took my hand and prayed with eyes very shut.

"Oh, Great Spirit of Jesus, come to our hearts to-day. White people think we pray to another god but we do not. We heard the talk of this white woman while we sat worshipping in our council tepee, and we have come out to pray for her.

Who made the sun? Who made these mountains? Who made this creek? Who made these trees and who brought the 'leetle woman' over here?

The Great God, our Father, that He may teach us more. She is your child. We are your children. We will call her no more white woman but sister.

How can we show that we believe you sent her ?

By saying thank you, thank you, thank you to Jesus ! We have spoken."

The prayers ended, the leader took me by the hand and followed by the other white robed figures, led me into the Ghost-Dance tepee and to the chief's seat.

The interior was exquisitely artistic and scrupulously clean.

The three beds, or sitting places, spread with brilliant blankets, were kept in place by thick ropes of tall grass twisted and tied with strips of gay calico.

The large square place in the middle of the tepee was as hard and as even as a cement floor.

The twenty-two tepee poles, clearly visible against the white canvas, were tied at the top with a lariat of braided buffalo hide and fastened to the ground near one of the beds with a strong crotched peg.

Hanging from one of these poles was a great bunch of eagle feathers, with quills elaborately beaded.

Gourds with beaded handles and primitive tom-toms lay here and there upon the beds, in front of which were carefully fashioned little wells for cuspidors about two inches deep and two wide.

There was no camp-fire, but in the exact centre of the tepee under the opening at the top a small piece of charcoal lay smouldering. A sprig of cedar was thrown upon it and when the place was filled with the aroma, tom-toms and gourds were brought into action, weird singing was engaged in and the pipe of peace passed. With the sign addressed to me: "You pray," all heads were bowed.

"Our Father in heaven, I don't know what it all means but I do know that I am not 'all alone and no scared' for Thou art with me. Teach me how to tell these poor people about Jesus and as they have walked in white with me to-day, so may they walk with Thee some day in the streets of the Beautiful City."

Four Indian prayers followed mingled with excessive weeping, and then I was led forth into the clear sunshine.

The man who acted as escort all the way through was the Mexican captive, Mokeen, beloved father of Lucius called Aitsan.

April 29th. At about nine o'clock to-night all who could, crowded into the large new Ghost-Dance tepee lately set up across Saddle Mountain Creek.

Praying and singing, beating the tom-toms, shaking the gourds and smoking to the Great Spirit continued for about two hours.

Then the blind medicine-man stood up and talked. When he was through a large woman, brilliantly painted and dressed, with quantities of black hair unbound, and rings and bracelets without number, arose and walking up to him, turned her back. Placing a hand on each shoulder he began gently swaying her from side to side, the motion increasing to such terrible rapidity that I thought the poor creature would surely break off at the waist.

With hair and arms flopping and eyes bulging out of her head, she finally fell, was lifted aside, and another victim took her place. Squirming, twisting men and women jumped up suddenly and sat down again. Beating of tom-toms, shaking of gourds and the minor wailing of song increased in discord as each new enquirer went forward.

All night this performance lasted, and in the morning after recovering their senses, each told of wonderful things seen, their dead children, the buffalo, Jesus, etc.

" The Great Father talked to us Himself," they said, "and told us He gave the Book to the White People and taught them to read it, but He gave to the Indians the dance road and told us to hold on to it tight till He came back to earth with our dead and our buffalo."

May 1st. They gave me an Indian name to-day : Gee-ah-hoan-go-mah, which means "She gave us the Jesus way."

May it prove prophetic.

May 10th. In the middle of the night I woke with a start.

Thunder rolled, lightning flashed, the tepee shook and the cot and myself were soaked through. Springing up I tried to find a place where the water was not pouring in but to none effect. Seizing the wet bedding I clapped it about me and, barefooted, sped up the hill to the house, where I mounted the kitchen table and steamed till morning.

At sunup, shivering and sneezing, I got back to the tepee before the Indians were about. Such a sight!

The pigs had been in and there wasn't a single thing except my Bible and Shakespeare that they had not upset, smashed, torn or eaten.

The dishes, pots and pans, etc., were scattered far and near. Five bars of soap, a package of tacks and a cake of stove polish were gone. The trunk that contained the provisions was ransacked and everything in it dragged out, scattered and destroyed. One bag of flour had been torn open under the cot, the other tramped into slush, with canned fruit, syrup, coal-oil and broken gem jars in front of it.

The oil-stove, with one leg off and three on,

had taken a header into the mess and on my appearance seemed to extend a cripple's welcome.

Scooping up enough clean flour and mixing it with water, I made up some kind of a dose to do for breakfast till we reached the store.

At about eleven o'clock the eighteen miles were covered and after filling up on canned stuff we started back with twenty-five dollars' worth of provisions.

May 11th. The pigs came in again in the night. Sawbeen, hearing them, came and waked me to give me a long pole she had made so that I could hammer them without getting up. I signed and told her I was too sick to fight pigs so she brought a quilt, spread it near the opening of the tepee, hung up a lantern and with the stick beside her, lay down to watch till morning.

May 12th. About midnight I was awakened again and told to hurry to the house for rain was coming. Lying on the table I made myself comfortable thinking of the man who got " bed and board for three dollars a week " but couldn't tell which was bed and which was board. At sunup I went back to the tepee.

History repeats itself. The pigs had been in of course and if they had done their best before

they certainly did their worst this time. Even
the trunk with the food, which had been locked
and placed on top of the cot, was smashed and
the cover lay under the bed bitten into kindling
wood. Every pick of food was gone, except
three cans of peas and they were bitten into
squashed shapes with here and there teeth marks
which let out the liquid. The cot was indescri-
bable. Pig! Pig! Pig!

May 13th. The tepee was moved this morning to a nice clean place up near the house. At
about ten o'clock I went out into the sunshine to
mix up bread batter on a biscuit box. Up
marched the three brutes in solemn procession
and made a regular charge at the pan. While
they pushed and squealed and grunted, I kicked
and shoved and tried to protect the stuff with my
arms, head and chest.

At an unguarded point the black pig stuck his
nose clear down into the bottom of the pan with
a whack. He got the whole mixture over the
back and ran off squealing and dripping. The
rest followed assisting with the music and inci-
dentally acted as breadwinners.

Five minutes later they were all back wear-
ing the most innocent determined Scotch ex-
pressions !

In the afternoon I went into my nice clean
tepee to try to get a little rest.

On a rope swung the mottoes:

"What would Jesus do?"

and

"Ask God to give thee skill
For comfort's art,
That thou mayest consecrated be,
And set apart unto a life of sympathy,
For heavy is the weight of ill in every heart —
And comforters are needed much
Of Christlike touch."

Closing my eyes and asking for the right kind of sympathy I fell into a gentle doze. Suddenly there was a bump-bump-bumping against the cot.

Jumping up, I grabbed something, saw the words: "What would Jesus do?" and "Of Christlike touch," and didn't hit them. I missed them all three!

May 18th. The home of Lucius Aitsan was a little two-roomed cottage with a large family bed on the floor in one room and a cot and a cookstove in the other. There were two tepees and an arbor in the yard.

Leading me into the house and standing by the stove Lucius said:

"You have had a hard time with pigs." (They had taken the notion to sleep beside my cot every night after pushing themselves under it innumerable times to scratch their backs.) "This room is yours. My wife cooks outside under the arbor in the summer time."

Coughing a big cough and sneaking a few tears down into my handkerchief I said : " The Great Father is kind. He prepares places in heaven and on earth for His children. This is good. Now let us go out and say thank you to your wife." (It was her brother Domot who had come to Elk Creek and invited me to Saddle Mountain.)

She was a little bit of a creature neat and clean, with an " honest Indian " face but so bashful she scarcely lifted her eyes from her screaming baby and the barking dogs.

In the evening by the light of a lantern hung amid the foliage of the arbor Lucius interpreted the Gospel to his people and afterwards told me the story of his life.

" When the elm trees turned red, near the Indian's New Year (spring) I was born.

The Kiowas and Utes were on the war-path camped at the head of the Canadian River, Indian Territory, and the Utes had burned To-haw-san's tepee. To-haw-san was government chief at the time.

My father, Mokeen, was a Mexican captive. He and an older brother were out looking for the milk cows when the Kiowas came upon them and carried him off. He was seven winters old and there were other captives. My mother was one of Santana's four wives. She had one son,

Odlepaugh. When her husband was killed she married my father.

The night I was born it was very cold. The buffalo tepee was in the timber on the river near a big red hill. Everybody was glad to see me and because I was a boy they painted my head and face yellow. If I had been a girl they would have painted me red.

'Heap of Bears,' the Indian they called my grandfather, was very much pleased with me and when an old Cheyenne Indian picked me up in his arms and kissed me he gave him a good black horse. I was a big brown baby with not much ' funny.'

A Blackfoot Indian on his way to visit his friends, the Cheyennes, fell in with the two war parties and was hiding along the river till he could get past. One night my grandfather saw him and called to him in the Cheyenne talk. Thinking he was a Cheyenne he came to him and when he was close enough my grandfather shot him. The Kiowas all thought this was very smart and they called me Aitsan, which means ' Killed-him-on-the-sly.'

My father and mother belonged to the Sun-Dance religion. Every summer ' Big Medicine ' councils were held and no water was drunk for three days and three nights.

When I was three years old my father took me in for half a day and gave me no water.

After that every summer I went to the Sun-Dance meetings and my father prayed that I might be a great man on the war-path, steal horses, kill and scalp people.

My mother loved me very much and took good care of me. I didn't run into other tepees a lot and she never let me stay away all day long. She made me a little buffalo skin tepee and I had a little donkey and a white dog with a red spot on top. When the camp moved the donkey carried my tepee and the little white dog. I began to learn to shoot at four winters old. When I was six my father brought home a buffalo calf and tied it to a tree. He showed me where to shoot and I hit it right on the heart and we all had a 'Big Eat.'

When I was nine Mr. Thomas Beaty came to start a school on Cache Creek and brought a big tent. One day I went in and was so surprised to see big pictures of all kinds of animals and fish. Mr. Beaty said the names in English and pointed to them and we tried to say the words after him. One day a woman ran in and carried her son out and my mother took me out too. They said we would die like the Caddos if we looked at those pictures.

Up to this time the Kiowas had never done any work except hunt. Government tried to make them but they wouldn't and when sheep were issued to them they ate them. At last the agent got some of the men to plough a field and plant it, but most of the Kiowas stood round watching and giving funny talk.

When the corn and melons came up and began to grow everybody was so surprised. Before the things were ripe they ate a lot and many took sick and died. My mother was one of them and after that I was very lonesome.

My father loved me just the same but a man can't take good care of a child. I was fourteen when my mother died. There was a school at Fort Sill then and I saw the children had such a good time that I wanted to go but my father wouldn't let me. I was big and would not mind, so after a while he got discouraged and let me go, October 10, 1878.

The first night I slept in a white man's house I was so happy I couldn't hardly sleep, because I had a chance to go to school. I learned to spell 'cat' the first day before noon. In the afternoon I could spell 'dog.' The second day I could spell 'a-b-c' and the next day 'd-e-f.' At the end of two weeks I knew cat, dog, cow, boy, pig, cup, and cap and the teacher said I was very 'smeart.' When the dinner bell rang I was so anxious to eat with a knife and fork.

In one moon my father came and asked me if I was lonesome and I said 'No, I am having a good time.' I was so proud of myself when I could say 'a-b-c' without the teacher.

The first Christmas tree surprised me very much and my heart hit very fast when they called my name on a red handkerchief and a monkey. When school was out in June lots of the boys and girls tore up their books and threw them away but I kept mine and read it.

That summer the agent wanted names to go away to Carlisle to school and Joshua Given and I gave ours when my father was out hunting horses. We both went to Fort Sill on one horse to give our names and I was awful skeered we would meet my father. When he heard he said: 'If you go I will kill myself.' But I said: 'I'm going anyhow.' He didn't think I would.

When I gave my name to Agent Hunt he said: 'I will take good care of your father,' so I knew it was all right. While we were in the office Hunting Horse came in with his little sister and said: 'I love my little sister but I want to send her to school,' and the tears fell on their cheeks. I looked at her and said: 'No use to send her away to school for she is such a little bit of a girl.' I felt sorry for her but I did not think to marry her then. Her mother was sitting outside crying. There were eleven of us wanted to go to school. The agent sent my father to Anadarko for freight and he went because he did not think I would go.

When we got started and were coming near Cache Creek I saw the freight wagons and the men staking their horses and I was awful skeered and wanted to hide but Joshua Given told me to sit still. My father saw me as he was bringing the horses up from the water and he dropped the rope and ran and took me in his arms and cried, and cried, and cried, and I cried too and nearly gave out. When he stopped crying he prayed to the sun and said, 'Oh, Sun! look upon my boy and let me see his face again!' Next morning he kissed me good-bye and when the wagons passed us I heard him crying—crying— awful hard.

At Anadarko the agent gave us letters to the chief clerk at Darlington and plenty of 'chuck.' When we got there Hunting Horse and Guechat went back and we were sent to Arkansas City to the railroad with some men who were freighting for the school.

When Soonday kissed her brother good-bye she cried and I thought: 'No use to send that poor little girl away to school.' Poor little Mabel—I never thought then that she would be my wife!

We were seven days on the road and it was awful cold. I wore a blanket but when I got up in the morning I was stiff. It was a cold, cold night when we got to Arkansas City. We camped across the bridge and made a fire out of sunflower weeds and slept out-of-doors.

In the morning the men took us to the station and a lot of white men ran calling, 'Here's the

Injins! Here's the Injins!' and we was 'shamed
for them. We heard the train coming a mile
from the station and we were so anxious to see
it, for we had never seen one. Captain Pratt
had telegraphed that he would be on the train
so we waited and when the track shook and the
engine ran past us we were all skeered. When
he got off we felt all right and looked at it all
over. After we were all in and the train began
to move I was 'fraid. The world went round
and my dinner got skeered and came up. At
Wichita Captain Pratt took us to an hotel, the
first one I was ever in. The table was so beautiful I was so proud of myself.

We waited three or four days for some
Cheyenne and Arapahoe boys and girls and I
got my hair cut. At Fort Sill they only cut it
on our shoulders but this time I had it cut like
the white men.

Then they took us into a room and brought in
a doctor and said if any of us were sick we would
have to go back. I was the first to stand before
the doctor and I was so skeered. He said:
'Pull off your shirt,' and then he hit me all over
and put his ear on me and heard that I was a
good healthy boy. Then Captain Pratt put
down my name and I was awful glad. There
were two who were sick and they begged awful
hard to go even if they died. Captain Pratt
gave them each five dollars and when we went

to the station with them we all cried, we felt so sorry for them.

We were three days on the train and were just like drunk.

After three years my time was up at Carlisle and I had to come back but I wanted to stay longer and learn more. They called me Lucius Ben Aitsan.

It was on the train coming back that I found out that I loved Mabel.

Mr. Weeks was an Episcopal minister at Anadarko and I went forward and had water put on my head and afterwards Mabel and I were married before him and Zotom.

After being assistant farmer at Anadarko one year I came to Saddle Mountain and located my farm and then went to Fort Sill and enlisted as a soldier. I was second sargeant and drank beer but did not gamble. I drank an awful lot of beer at first and was sick in bed. After, I only drank a little at a time. When I was in Anadarko Boton said to me: 'Come to the Catlick Church and see wonderful things in all the world.' They asked me to interpret and I got up to do it but the man talked so fast in some talk I did not understand that I asked to be excused and sat down. They had candles and images and when they passed before Jesus they went as if they were going to sit down.

After that I interpreted the Gospel for Dr.

Murrow and the other missionaries and hid all their wise talks in my heart.

I never told anybody but I have been asking Jesus on the sly to send a Jesus woman to our district and to my home that I might learn more. There was a man just like me in the Bible. He believed the best way he knew how and Jesus knew it and sent a man to ride with him who explained everything so plainly that he understood and was baptized. There are no Christians here. The Indians all live in camps scattered along the different creeks. We have no 'Jesus day' and nothing special to live for but ourselves. I have spoken."

May 24th, Sunday. It was the same "old story" that was told and the same questions that were asked :

" Are there any Christians present ? "

" Are there any who would like to be ? "

Indian politeness made an answer necessary and a dignified, thoughtful reply was given.

"There are no Christians here. We worship a different way. The news you have brought is very wonderful, but Indians do not hurry to pick up new roads. We must take time to think it over carefully and then we will give you our answer."

After dinner a second meeting was held and a second time the invitation was given.

"Are there not some of you who would like to have this great loving Saviour for your Friend?"

Immediately there arose from the ground an old, old, old woman, very stooped and so brown and wrinkled that the human visage was almost obliterated. Over the top of her dilapidated Indian clothing she had put on a dress from a missionary barrel that had belonged to a child about ten years of age.

Her scrawny arms were poked through the sleeves and the garment was partly drawn up on the shoulders. The skirt did not reach to the knees and the feet were covered with one white and one black stocking.

Never in all my life had I seen a more ludicrous object.

As she scrambled from the ground rigged in this awful combination, not a smile nor a leer was visible on a single face and Lucius interpreted as though she had been a chief's wife in gorgeous apparel.

This is what she said:

"I am the oldest woman here and I will make a talk.

I never heard anything like it before and I can't tell you to-day whether I believe it or not but we thank you. I have lived many winters and have seen much trouble. My husband is dead and my daughters who are living have many children. My work is to carry their papooses on my back every day, when they are sick and when they are well.

I am often tired and hungry for rest.

When you told us this morning about that Beautiful Home with water and fruit and no more 'hungry and crying,' and the Kind Chief who wanted to divide up with everybody, I thought, that is the kind of a place that would suit me. I didn't get up in the meeting for I wanted to think about it some more.

I understand if we pick up this new road we must dress like white people so I have put on this dress to let everybody know that if I can have this Jesus as my Friend and go to live with Him after I get through with this life, I am willing to go round like this the few winters that are left, even if all my people think that I am crazy. It is a wonderful road. I have spoken."

Elk Creek is about forty miles from Saddle Mountain. It was to this point that the Society sent me with Miss Everts in the fall of ninety-three. It was here also that we enjoyed many unusual experiences.

Experience No. 1 :

While holding a meeting in camp one day a white man arrived with a load of turkeys. They were seventy-five cents a piece, but as he too was a Baptist he said he would give us ours for fifty cents.

"Can you change a dollar?" I asked, and receiving an affirmative answer, skipped up to the house while he went to the wagon for the turkey.

After it was tethered I handed over the dollar.

Pulling *a quarter* from his pocket the man exclaimed, "Well! I sure thought it was a fifty cent piece. The turkey is big though and worth seventy-five cents."

That night he camped on the other side of the creek. Before sunrise I was up, waded across, handed back the quarter and said :

"I sure am a Baptist and have decided to take *two* turkeys instead of one." He laughed uproariously as he handed over the second bird.

Experience No. 2 :

We had run out of wood and it was bitter cold. With a rope slung round my neck I crossed the creek at the same place and was returning with a fine load of fallen timber on my back when something happened. In scrambling up the bank, briars tangled in my skirts and over went every stick into the creek and floated off.

Experience No. 3 :

Miss Everts was nearly starved and when I teased her about it big round tears appeared. Flying out of the door she said : "If you were as hungry as I am you would cry too."

For penance I decided to take some of the Lord's time next day and go a-fishing.

In the same creek at the same crossing I fished from eleven to twelve, from twelve to one, from one to two and from two to three and never got a bite:

June 24th. We had all come over from Saddle Mountain to Elk Creek to the camp-meeting and Lucius was doing part of the interpreting.

There are always converts ready for baptism before the meetings begin, so the first thing that the ministers do after the opening services, is to invite these to the front.

As Lucius gave the invitation he stepped forward and turning his back to the audience joined in the singing.

A little woman at the far end of the arbor arose with a baby on her back and came slowly forward.

He did not see her till she stood beside him and then bursting into tears he sobbed: "She is my wife," and could interpret no more.

June 28th. It was Sunday afternoon and a long brilliant procession moved slowly towards the illustrious spot on Elk Creek.

Children gaily attired climbed up into the trees, men on horseback wrapped in blankets of all hues leaned forward, and women, some with babies on their backs, stood and sat in their graceful draperies with faces livid with joyful anticipations.

Then there echoed up and down the waterside, in English, broken English and Kiowa gutturals :

> " O happy day that fixed my choice
> On Thee, my Saviour and my God."

How they sang it and how the tears in many eyes showed they felt it !

> " He taught me how to *wash* and pray,
> And live rejoicing every day."

And their clean clothing and happy faces told the same story.

Some one prayed and then Rev. H. H. Clouse's voice was heard above the singing of the birds and the ripple of the water :

" On profession of your faith and in obedience to our Lord's command, I baptize thee, Lucius Aitsan, into the name of the Father, Son and Holy Ghost."

> " Happy day, happy day
> When Jesus washed my sins away."

" On profession of your faith, and in obedience to our Lord's command, I baptize thee, Mabel Aitsan, into the name of the Father, Son and Holy Ghost."

Hand in hand they came up out of the water with "Happy day, happy day" trembling upon their lips.

Reaching down to help them up the slippery bank of the historic creek, past experiences became obliterated, and I felt that it paid to endure hardness even as a *poor* soldier of Jesus Christ.

July 8th. " DEAR MISS CRAWFORD: I write briefly to say that at the meeting of the Executive Board held yesterday the ladies voted to allow you to remain at Saddle Mountain as long as it is *safe* and *prudent* and also to allow you $12.50 per month for an interpreter.

·" MARY G. BURDETTE."

August 1st. Vacation.

II

Experiences—Church Building Fund—Death— Ploughing—An Indian Function—Camp- meeting

NOVEMBER 27, 1896.   Chickasha !
   In a few minutes I was standing on the platform.
Such a greeting !

The three yellow dogs didn't know me and barked.   Carlo did know me and growled.   The baby shrieked.   Jessie clung to her mother's blanket.   Mabel smiled and looked down.

Only Lucius was brave enough to take me by the hand and shake it.   He was the chief !

While busy "loading up" six cows tore open the tent at the edge of the town eating the hay in the beds, so it was a sorry looking place they took me to but it could not be helped.

Scraping up what there was left and producing from a bag two new sheets and a pillow-case, Lucius proceeded to make a "white-man's bed" for me.   Then he made a big wide one at the other side of the tent for himself and family and pulling up two pegs slept with his head outside.

November 30th.   We reached Saddle Moun- tain chilled to the marrow bones to start out again for a government payment at Rainy Mountain.

December 13th. Haven't had my clothes off since coming into camp two weeks ago.

Forty children from the Government School were baptized to-day in Rainy Mountain Creek, among them Amos Aitsan and a little Indian maiden named Kaun-todle, the daughter of a white woman captured in infancy and married into the tribe.

December 14th. Home again.

December 15th. Company—company—company pouring in from every direction. There isn't standing room in the house, morning, noon or night—cold.

December 16th. More company. It is a continuous reception, hard on the constitution but full of opportunities.

December 17th. It was so cold last night in the kitchen that I couldn't sleep, and this morning Lucius and Mabel moved my bed into their room and put it across a window (the only place there was for it), and I put up a curtain allowing one foot for dressing room.

December 18th. Helping with the dishes this morning I noticed that the guests were leaving, so scooping the greasy dish-water from my arms

I said : " Lucius ! It won't do to let all these people go home without any *spiritual* food," and for one hour we told them about Jesus with arms akimbo as the grease dried in.

I'm a believer in a consecration that goes in at prayer and comes out at dish-water and suds, a consecration that will tackle the meanest kind of work for His sake and not shove it off on somebody else or sneak out of it altogether.

Digging into downright disagreeable work often has more real worship in it than hours of secret prayer.

December 25th, Christmas. Everybody away. Observed Lent and kept mum.

January 1, 1897. Gave the camp a grand New Year dinner to-day, making everybody help with the work. They were greatly interested in the *cleaning, washing* and *picking over* of the things for the plum pudding, but when everything was stirred together in a pan, tied up in a cloth and plumped into a pot of boiling water their faces went blank !

The thing had been drowned—and in hot water !

Some of them signing " It-is-a-heap-crazy-road " marched out the door and held a council about it in the yard.

The menu consisted of roast chicken, rabbit potpie, beans, dried apples, cranberries, bread, currant buns, tapioca pudding, plum pudding, pop-corn, candy, tea and coffee.

How I was tempted to put "some strong medicine" or coal-oil on the pudding and set it afire !

At first they tasted it as if afraid of being burned or poisoned but it wasn't long before they were shovelling it down in great spoonfuls, calling it "Sweet-chuck-in-a-rag."

After the feast the thirty-one guests crowded into the other room and listened reverently to the story of the man who went to a wedding without a clean blanket on. At night when I crept to sleep, the floors covered with mud and Indians, my mind ran from a cup of cold water to a plum pudding given in His name.

January 6th. Sick-a-bed with a cold or cold-a-bed with a sick. The wind fairly whistles about my head.

January 8th. Got up at noon and made an invention. Pulling the cot out from the wall I opened an umbrella on it, threw a big blanket over the whole thing, pushed the bed back tight against the window, crawled back into place, held on to the handle and Eureka ! The canopy top worked like a charm !

From Greenland's icy mountain to India's coral strand, waft, waft, ye winds, but you don't waft on me any more! (Unless the thing blows overboard in the night.)

The family went down to the camp on the creek and I got up. The stove was so dirty I cleaned it, the sink was so greasy I scoured it, the floor was dusty I swept it. Then I cooked something I thought I could eat and three Indians came in to dinner.

January 10th–18th. Company! company! company!

January 19th.

" Give me a calm, a thankful heart, from every murmur free,
The blessing of Thy grace impart and let me live for Thee."

January 20th. Cold and company.

" Give me a calm, a thankful heart, from every murmur free,
The blessing of Thy grace impart and let me live for Thee."

January 21st. Company and cold.

" Give me a calm, a thankful heart, from every murmur free,
The blessing of Thy grace impart and let me live for Thee."

I was hungry and thought when I saw the

nice fresh beef the Indians brought that I would make a little Irish stew for myself in my own granite pot.

It smelled so good as it simmered all morning on the back of the stove.

I worked at letters till the rest were all through dinner and then went out to get mine. The cover was off the pot and it was swilling over with refuse from the plates!

I didn't want a "calm and thankful heart" just then—I wanted Irish stew! There were twenty-seven to dinner.

January 26th. At noon to-day as soon as the wagon stopped I bounded out with my biscuit-box suit-case and made for the woods.

Undressing I donned a missionary barrel tea-gown with a "Wateau back," hung my clothing on a tree, grabbed the biscuit box, the washboard and a bar of soap and escaped to the creek, in drapery outrivaling the Goddess of Liberty in New York harbor.

Planting the biscuit box bottom side up in the water, I sat down fast on it and the bundle of soiled clothes.

Holding the washboard between my knees, piece by piece I pulled the things from under me and after the rubbing and scrubbing let each drift down-stream to do its own rinsing. Washboard, soap and box were then thrown to the bank and seizing myself by the "Wateau back" I rescued the garments and strung them all out on the bushes to dry. They were ironed while I quietly sat on them giving the "Jesus talk" after the camp dinner.

Domot made this talk:

"When I was a young man we had plenty of buffalo. We made our tepees, our clothing and our bedding out of the skin. We got our bowstrings out of the sinew. We made medicine out of the fat and had plenty to eat and the dogs were never hungry.

Thirty years ago the white soldiers came and they shot and shot and shot and killed and killed and killed big and little, leaving the bodies and skins to rot.

In seven years our buffalo were all gone and to-day we are poor and hungry.

White men are kill-crazy. The buffalo they kill, kill, kill. Indians they kill, kill, kill. Jesus they killed. What's the matter? Why? Why? Why?"

Taboodle is perhaps ninety years old. I was giving him a long, earnest talk when he put up his hands and signed:

"Wait! A question I want to ask. Why is it that some white men have no-hair-on-top and others have a-heap-on-their-chins?"

January 28th. Although Lucius and Mabel

do not know when they were born they have kept track of their children's birthdays.

Wee Sarah is two years old to-day and besides a " Big Eat," she received a dime for candy and an envelope containing a gold dollar and a Canadian ten-cent piece to be put by, as a starter, for a church at Saddle Mountain.

The gold dollar was given me at the end of my first year in the Training School by Miss Henrietta Wright of Chicacole, India.   The Canadian ten-cent piece was presented at my graduation by Miss Burdette with the remark : " It belongs to the Queen.   I have no use for it.   Take it back and spend it."

When " Liberty " and " The Queen " put their heads together something is sure to happen.

February 1st.   Ah-to-mah, hearing about the gold dollar and dime, sent ten cents for the building fund, making it $1.20.   " We must keep quiet about this," said Lucius, " or the Kiowas will all kick."

Excitement ran high when the news got out, for it had been decided long ago that no church or anything else " white " should be built in the vicinity.   When men brought lumber to Sugar Creek to build a Government School Papedone and others got on their horses with guns and drove them back.   The school was afterwards built at Rainy Mountain.

Ah-to-mah's husband sent word if lumber for a church was brought in he would get up in the night and throw it in a ditch.

February 4th. A big prairie schooner halted at our door and an Indian man and woman got out. The man was tall and slightly built, his gorgeous blanket falling in graceful folds giving him a strikingly picturesque appearance.

The woman was tall and thin also, with such a sad face. From her right hand one finger had been chopped, the silent witness of the death of a near and dear one. Tightly held on her back by a brilliant blanket of yellow, green, blue and black was the emaciated form of a little girl about five years of age in the last stage of consumption.

They had heard of the arrival of a Jesus woman at Aitsan's camp and after everything else had failed, came with their sick and their broken hearts.

The horses were hobbled and turned loose, a tepee was set up in the yard and life went on apparently as usual.

In another tepee down on the creek all was joy and rejoicing, for to a father and mother with but one son and five daughters a little boy baby was born. He was given the name Clark Preston, for one whose locks, character and soul were as white as the driven snow.

On the afternoon of February 16th, as the sun

was sinking behind the hills, I entered the tepee to see this little one take three breaths and die.

The sting of death is the same the world over, and these stricken parents after placing the lifeless body in my arms gave themselves over to uncontrollable weeping. Mingling my tears with theirs I signed: "Jesus has taken your child to sit down with Him. He does not want you to cut off your fingers. He wants you to give your hearts to Him."

The only box that would make a coffin was full of chips. Emptying it I made a lid, lined and covered the whole with white, and printed across the top: "Not dead, but living with Jesus."

The interpreter was away but the wonderful resurrection story was signed into the hearts, bringing for the moment a holy calm.

After prayer I took up the hammer.

The wailing broke out afresh to such an extent that I put it down and in my helplessness prayed again—this time for myself—that strength might be given.

The sobbing ceased, the cover was replaced, the nails were driven and soon a wagon containing the coffin, an Indian man and woman, three hoes and myself, drove rapidly out of the camp.

Under a lone tree at the foot of the mountain the little grave was fashioned. When all was ready, the coffin resting on the mother's orange and green blanket, heads were bowed and a prayer offered to Him who once stood beside an open grave and wept.

The casket was lowered on the blanket, the Indian holding two corners and the woman and myself the other two. The little one's belongings were all dropped in. A pause followed.

Gathering up a handful of the soil and signing to the others to do the same, together, on our knees, we sprinkled in the finest of the earth till the last bright folds of the blanket were lost to sight and then we worked with the hoes.

The sun had sunk to rest, bathed in a living glory and the sad moon had climbed the neighboring hills ere our mournful task was ended. In neither light could there be seen, north, south, east or west, a church spire pointing to Him who said : " I am the resurrection and the life."

I was sitting lost in study the following Monday evening when softly the door opened and the Indian in the yard whose little daughter lay sick of a fever stood before me and signed : "My child will die to-morrow. The Great Father is kind. There are too many in my tepee. May some come and sleep in the house?"

The interpreter and his family were gone to the agency but I signed, "Yes," and then hastened to make up beds on the floor.

At daylight I hurried to the tepee and found the mother bending over her child with face as motionless as death. The father was staining a little buckskin dress the brightest shade of yellow.

When he came in to breakfast his nostrils dilated rapidly, his eyes were vacant and his lips protruded.

"Let the Lord do what seemeth good in His sight," was the morning lesson.

When he understood it he signed : "The Great Father knows what is best. I do not. My heart is sore." And covering his head all over he bowed for prayer.

Five minutes later a woman rushed in and signed : "The child is dead. Hurry and make the coffin."

Entering the tepee I found it was true. The Spirit had flown, leaving the warm clay in the arms of the distracted mother.

Another box was emptied and made strong but there were no boards long enough for a cover, so short ones had to be joined and made into correct proportions.

Why didn't the Indians do the work?

Death, to those who have never or lately heard the Gospel, is terrifying. Superstition makes them want to fly from every semblance of it.

In a panic it is not easy to get control. The child had to be buried. I made the coffin and went to the tepee.

Was it life or was it death that I beheld?

On a cream colored shawl, with a border of scarlet roses, in the buckskin dress of yellow, the body lay. Around the neck were numberless strings of beads, bracelets encircled the wrists, rings the fingers, and clasped in the arms was a brightly attired rubber doll. The face—could it be death?

Where were the ashy pallor, the closed eyes, the compressed lips? Gone—not a semblance of death was there. The hair and face were tinted " like the yellow leaves in autumn," the cheeks, ears, division of hair and lips were brilliant red, the eyes were wide open and the lips parted.

The parents' lips were colored also!

At the funeral there were no demonstrations of grief, save now and then a tear would fall and the parents' heads sink nearer the coffin.

A wagon stood at the door. Helping the mother in I sat beside her on the precious box. Two men and eight women (all who were in camp) followed with a long piece of canvas and several hoes.

Within a short distance of the lone tree the mother gave a wild shriek and threw herself over the coffin. Her keen eye had discovered that wolves and coyotes had scraped down into the other little grave and had it not been for the rude coffin the body would have been dragged out and eaten.

Making the grave was a long, hard process, for below the surface we struck a stratum of clay that had to be chopped into chunks and lifted out in the piece of canvas.

Everybody worked except the mother and there were times when all were so exhausted that we sank on the heap of soil, with backs to the bitter wind, and waited till our strength returned.

At last the sad task was ended (the father placing two wagon loads of rock upon the grave to keep the wolves out).

The sun was high in the heavens, his bright rays falling upon the cold stone pile, but nowhere, though he penetrated mountain top and valley, could he find a monument reared to Him who said: "I am the resurrection and the life."

Returning, the parents cut their hair, laid aside their bright wrappings, burned the tepee, covered the camp-fire and one behind the other disappeared up the mountainside.

At sunrise I found the mother sitting beside the covered camp-fire in the yard, the picture of desolation, wailing, wailing, wailing with her face turned towards the lone tree.

If the loss of a child can bring such terrible anguish what of the loss of a soul?

April 6th. Ploughing is the order of the day. Six of the nearest of kin have clubbed and are

ploughing one field at a time.   They finish here
to-day.

When they came in to dinner all were " heap
tired " and then they were " heap mad " because
I hid the cake till dessert time.

" All white people have the ' hide-road,' " they
signed, and then sat so long at the table discuss-
ing the point that I produced the baking-powder
can and heaping up a teaspoonful, told one of
them to open his mouth.

He signed : " Why ?   What for ? "

I signed :

" It will help you rise."

The pouts departed and the ploughing went
on.   During the day a company of soldiers
guarding the money wagons galloped past, wav-
ing " Old Glory " over their heads, and at night
this question was asked :

" Why didn't the government tell us about the
other life in heaven ? "

" We didn't know it was Jesus who wanted us
to plough.   We thought it was the white men
and we wouldn't do it."

April 8th.   Couldn't stand it any longer so
went out and signed to an Indian : " The Great
Father has watched you sit under this arbor
three days doing nothing but eat and talk.   If
He had made the road for you to do just these
two things He would have made you all mouth

and stomach, no hands, no legs, no feet, just one big 'chuck bag.' He put hands and feet on you so that you could take hold of a plough and walk after it." He signed : "When I plough my heart hurts me. My hands and feet are strong but my heart hits fast." I replied, "You would be dead if it did not hit." He went to work.

In the evening I gave this talk to the camp :

"The Great Father wants us to work with Him. He made the seed and put life in it. White men could make something that would look like corn but they couldn't put life in it and it wouldn't come up. When you plant the Great Father's seed He sends the sun and the rain to encourage you and makes it grow. He does the hardest part. If you love Him you will try to please Him and do yours. He could have sent 'women-with-wings' (angels) to plough for you and carry the Gospel to others but He did not.

What would we do to show Him that we love Him if angels did everything? He wants you to plough and to plant and give the spiritual seed to others and He promises to take good care of you all the way along. Those who ploughed to-day have made His heart glad."

"The Great Father didn't give the work road," called out Mokeen.

"Long time ago God gave a garden to a white man and woman and they didn't have to work, they just had to look after things. Then these white people went crazy in their hearts and began to steal, and the Great Father turned them off and told them to work till the water ran down their backs. They went on the war-path and killed everybody till they were taken captives.

Long time ago God gave Indians land and they didn't steal. Their hearts were good every day, every day, every day. They didn't have to work either, but just hunt buffalo. After a while crazy white men came and stole all the buffalo and gave them the work road. Then they went on the war-path and killed everybody till they were beaten. White people are heap crazy. The Great Father didn't give the work road."

"When me and Jesus was out ploughing," said Poor Buffalo, "the devil got mad and put a piece of barbed wire before us. It cut my hand. The blood came but I did not get mad. I sat right down and told the Great Father about it. Then I tore a piece off my shirt, tied up my hand and me and Jesus went on with the work."

"I don't beg all the time," said another. "I ask once and wait. I am too old to plough. The Great Father understands. Sometimes He gives me a coat or a pant, but when He does not I go ahead just the same. If I die with no coat or pant on Jesus will take me to live with Him and I won't need anything to put on there."

Heenkey had a question to ask : "One thing I want to know. Does the Jesus Book say any

place that the Kiowa Indians are to have one
hundred and sixty acres of land apiece? Jesus
never told us this. It is the white men. The
Great Father made the land and put us on it and
we love the land our Great Father gave us.

It makes my heart sick when we hear that
white men want to come in here. The missionaries must help us to keep them out. Many of
them are very wicked and they will give us bad
roads. Pray for us that we may keep our land.
I have spoken."

"Plough! Heenkey, plough! Plough! Everybody plough!

The Great Father gave you the land *to work*,
and He will supply the seed and the sunshine and
the rain and make things grow.

If you don't do it others will get your land.
Work! work! work! everybody work! It is the
best way to keep the white people off."

Copied from the *Chikasha Express:*

" These full-bloods should be given the opportunity to go to some other country if they want
to. Almost any country would welcome them
with open arms. They are first-class citizens at a
shooting-match or at a game of monte or make
a full hand at loafing, but as a benefactor in
making two spears of grass grow where one grew
before they are a failure.

Let them go. Let the government buy their
land it gave them and then drive them to some

other country if any other country will take them They have been pests and scabs long enough."

April 14th. We were all invited to Lucius' brother's tepee to supper to-night.

Ananthy sat at the end of the bed nearest the entrance with everything beside her. When all were seated three narrow lengths of white oilcloth were passed, followed quickly by granite plates and cups, some knives, forks and spoons, the coffee-pot, a can of fruit and two white wash basins of beef.

When the meal was over, each stacked his and her own dishes and with the oilcloths and refuse sent them back to Ananthy. Water, soap and flour-sack towels were next sent up the line, and after I had used them passed on down to the others.

While the finger-bowl was going the rounds our hostess was busy washing the dishes and putting things away. In an incredibly short time she was all through with hands and face washed and hair smoothed.

Bravo! She had served that whole meal from beginning to end without taking one single step!

Fresh logs were added to the camp-fire, the pipe of peace was passed from mouth to mouth and then Montgomery Ward's catalogue was produced triumphantly. Something was coming! Opening it at the *underwear* department our host signed :

"Why? Why? Why aren't those white women 'shamed to stand up and have their pictures took that way? Kiowa women wouldn't do it."

When this puzzling question was explained to the satisfaction of all he proceeded :

" Before white people came we were happy all the time and seldom got mad.

The Great Father gave us the buffalo and we had plenty to eat. We don't like the white man's pork and now when we are hungry we get mad quick and want to fight.

Old Odlepaugh was a war chief. My father gave me his name. When he got mad he bit the noses off his wives. He bit them off three and turned them loose. Nobody wanted to marry 'women-with-noses-got-none,' and the chief's heart was full (satisfied).

When we went on the war-path we rode till the food gave out and then ate our horses.

We were looking for just one thing—white men, and when we found them we fought them hard. We were kind to the women and children.

When we captured Mokeen he cried and cried and cried."

"Stop! stop! wait!" signed Mokeen from across the fire. "He gives you lies. I was brave. Some of the Indians were bad, their hearts were like stones, they took white papooses by the legs and threw them up in the air as far as they could, and then rubbed dirt into their faces.

"They had no sense. I have spoken." Odlepaugh continued :

"Once a war party returned with three white women captives. Old Tassat stood with them, and while we danced in a circle round them she hit them with sticks to make them jump. They cried and cried and cried, louder and louder and louder and fell down. They tried to get away but Tassat wouldn't 'cut off.' White men had killed her son; she would pay them back.

We sold these women afterwards to the Mexicans for corn bread. They would not cook for us.

It is time now for you to go to bed. We have told you these 'long-time-ago-roads' to make you see in your sleep" (dream).

I signed: "Wait till I tell you a story I want you to see in your sleep too," and fresh logs were piled upon the fire.

Sinner that I was, I sat by that blazing campfire till long after midnight telling the awful story of "Ali Baba and the Forty Thieves." And I did it, knowing that Miss Burdette was raising my poor little salary by telling the people how dear Miss Crawford was carrying the Gospel to the poor Indians from tepee to tepee amid great privations and hardships !

When the story was finished there was a dead

pause, for they had been under a sort of spell clear through.

I am not sure but that they will mix the forty thieves with the twelve apostles and seventy elders, and swallow the whole absurd story as part of the Gospel, but if they do they won't be any farther off the track than some preachers I know and they will be a great deal easier to get back on again.

May 3d, Sunday. Doybi gave fifty cents to the church and Barking Wolf fifty in handiwork. Building fund, $2.20.

May 5th. The white visitors have gone.

Dr. Murrow is the first Baptist Jesus-man to preach a sermon in this district.

There was so much cleaning and cooking getting ready for the company that the pleasure of it was somewhat marred by "tired."

Last night after all were in bed I sneaked to the chicken house and helped to pick two hens. Before going to sleep I remembered that the lard pail was empty and we were twenty miles from a store. Sunrise found me down among the tepees looking for grease and grace.

We had fried chicken for breakfast, followed by prayers, hand-shaking and good-byes.

I wonder when I really prayed last? We have had from nine to thirty-nine every meal the winter through.   It seems a long time since I prayed prayerfully but I'm sure I've worked prayerfully and I don't honestly believe the prayer from the company this morning would have come so straight from the heart if there hadn't been fried chicken in the stomach!

May 6th.   Teams started for lumber for a new room and food.

May 9th.   Awful rains.   Lucius not back, nothing to eat but salt and flour.

May 10th.   This afternoon I heard thump-thump-thump-bumpety-bump under the house and awful dog barking and pup yelping.   Going out I found Mabel with a long board poking for all she was worth.

Asking her what was the matter she signed:

"Lucius comes not, all are hungry, the pups I will kill and eat."

I said, "Mabel!   You are not going to eat those pretty little yellow pups, are you?"

She signed: "Yes," and I went in.

When the barking ceased I went out again and signed: "Mabel, if you will cut off two of the hind legs of one of the pups, skin them so there won't be a hair left, wash them and put them on a clean plate, I believe I am hungry enough to eat them."

It was done as requested and I helped to eat

the beautiful yellow pups, the heart-broken mother barking and whining the whole time.

June 19th. A wagon came this morning to take me down the creek about two miles where an arbor has been built for the camp-meeting.

As we drove up four men and four women knelt in prayer with torn clothing and blistered and bleeding hands.

When they had finished they signed : " It is done. We have told Jesus about it in our poor way. We have sent for you to come and tell Him good that He may thoroughly understand that we did all this work for Him because we want more souls saved."

June 27th–July 1st. Camp-meeting.

> " Hark ! hark, the dogs do bark !
> The tinkers are coming to town ! "

Returned missionaries look bad enough in pulpits, but if the congregations could only see us now ! Mother Hubbards, Father Hubbards, overalls and rompers ! Red beards, white beards, blue beards and stubble ! Sunbonnets, rain coats, goggles and tan ! Black ties, white ties and " blest-be-the-ties ! " Hark ! hark, the dogs do bark ! and I don't blame them.

A few years ago the Arapahoe Sitting Bull gave the " Ghost-Dance-road " to the Indians and the Kiowa tribe sent Ahpeatone to make investigations. He took with him many gifts from the tribe and reaching the encampment enquired the way to Jesus' tepee. Six men accompanied him and entering found " Jesus " lying on an Indian bed, wrapped in a white sheet with his bare feet exposed.

Expressing sorrow that some of the women had not made him a pair of pretty moccasins, Ahpeatone explained the object of his coming : The Kiowa tribe had heard that Jesus had returned to earth and after He had visited all the tribes was going to give back their dead and their buffalo. Was it true?

When " Jack Wilson," the half-breed Jesus, sat up and threw his sheet back, Ahpeatone left the tepee and returning to the tribe reported the whole Ghost-Dance movement " one big lie."

Finding his younger brother he said :

" Tonemoh, I have tried all the religions of the tribe ; they are short ; none of them lead through. The Jesus road is the true road ; look for it till you find it and pick it up. I have two wives and cannot put my feet on it."

At the close of the camp-meeting eighteen professing Christians were baptized in Saddle Mountain Creek, Tonemoh among the number, (a future deacon).

" I have nothing to give you to make your heart happy," said Popebah as I was leaving for vacation, "but I send my best love to your mother because she did not keep you at home."

Poor Indians! Surely any "creature" capable of understanding a mother's love in giving a daughter can comprehend a Father's love in giving a Son.

August 1st. Vacation.

Building fund, $2.20. (Treasurer, Mrs. H. Stevens, Dayton, Ohio.)

III

*The Coming of Miss McLean—A Death-Blow—
The Gospel Tent—Four Scenes—Organiza-
tion of Missionary Society—Big Eats—An
Important Message*

1897.

I WAS sitting in the Presbyterian Church in Ionia, Michigan, one Sunday evening in the summer of '92, when I saw the face of a woman I had not seen for years.

We had known each other in North Dakota, she had moved away, and long after we had returned to Canada.

Next day I sat quietly nearly half an hour in her company, while a friend kept up a conversation, before making myself known.

I told her I felt sure that God had brought us together again that she might hear about the Training School and go to it.

She went, and from the very first wrote of her desire to come and help me after graduation.

" I cannot do the missionary part of the work," she wrote, " but I'm sure I can take some of the responsibilities off your shoulders."

When there was a room to live in I wrote to the Board asking that Miss Mary McLean be sent to Saddle Mountain.

The Rock Island train was unexpectedly switched off into "Siding No. 1," one station above Chickasha and five masked men got on board, lined the passengers up along a barbed wire fence and ordered: " Hands up !"

The men were all robbed except Father Isadore of Anadarko, the safe blown open and the desperados escaped to the mountains.

(The conductor lost his watch and chain, but advertising for the return of the locket, as it contained the picture of his mother, he got it.)

Reward notices for the capture of these robbers were posted all along the line as Miss McLean and I were carried past " Siding No. 1 " into Chickasha the morning of October 7, 1897.

October 24th. The Sunday service under the arbor was a sort of reception. How glad the Indians were to see two of us. But some hearts were sad. Saing-poh, who had said under the same arbor in the spring: " If the Great Father brings you back again we will see each other with no trouble," was present with empty arms. Her only little one was gone.

October 25th. Domot, the father, called with hair all cut and lips quivering.

Dropping his head gently upon my shoulder he wept silently for some time and then signed : " My little girl is dead. Jesus has carried her up.

I have lost many children and have always been afraid when they died. This time I'm not afraid. You have told me the true road. I know now that my little ones are with Jesus. He knows what is best. I am not afraid but my heart cries."

November 10th. Rainy Mountain Mission. Camp-meeting.

Miss Reeside was cleaning the stove, Miss Ballew doctoring the sick, Miss McLean making an Indian dress and I was cleaning the windows when word was brought in that Challinone was dying. (The pastor was off to the railroad for the guests but he had left the rough wooden casket ready in the barn.) Hastening to the tepee we found it full of waiting relatives and friends. Miss Reeside prayed. There were a few short gasps and all was over.

If "wonderful" can be used in describing a funeral it certainly is the word to be used here.

After Miss Reeside and Miss Ballew had made their talks Big Tree shambled up to the coffin and picking up the dead man's hand bowed over the face and sobbed: "Oh my friend! This is the last time I shall hold your hand till you hold it out to me in the Home above. You and I played together as children, as young men we went on the war-path, together we found the Jesus road and together we have worked to save our people.

My beloved friend, tell Jesus I will not grow tired of His way. I will ——"

He could speak no further and standing by the coffin with face turned to heaven, his great form shook with sobs. Challinone had requested that his "medicine-bag" should be buried with him as he did not wish to hand down the "old religion" to his children.

It was Sainco who said: "Let us put a Bible under his head with the 'medicine-bag' under his feet. It was the 'good medicine' that cured his heart."

November 13th. I had had no mail for weeks. An Indian brought a flour sack full. There were two letters from home.

My mother died October 25th !

Her last poem :

> I read that trees have tongues,
> That a voice is granted them
> To cheer and give instructions
> To us foolish mortal men.
>
> I walked alone through the forest
> In December chill and cold,
> When the lovely form of nature
> Was wrapped in a snowy fold.
>
> As I stood 'neath the naked branches
> Sad were the tears I shed,
> For I thought when I saw them leafless
> That the forest trees were dead.

Above the wild storm a sharp shrill sound
Rose sad on the bitter breeze,
And I heard these words of wisdom pass
From the quaking forest trees :

" We are living, dear friend, we are living,
Though the semblance of death we bear,
We but wait for a brighter season
To resume our foliage fair.

And birds shall sing 'neath our branches
And violets 'neath us bloom
When our verdure burst with gladness
Cold winter's icy tomb.

Oh, be like us and remember
In the solemn hour of death
That a glorious resurrection
Shall follow a life of faith."

November 14th. Coming sadly out of my tent this morning I was surrounded by a number of old Indian men wrapped in faded blankets.

They had laid aside their bright colors to show sympathy in their own way.

Placing a brown arm about me and pressing my aching head upon his shoulder (*as he had placed his own on mine the very day my mother died*) Domot prayed while the others cried aloud. " O Great Spirit ! Our leetle Jesus woman has lost her mother and her heart is all broken to pieces. Gather it together again and put it back strong. You have given her to us now and we will take the best care of her we know how. That is all. I have spoken."

How I cried!

The brown arm and nasty blanket were repulsive to me. The whole life was horrid. I hadn't a taste in common with it. I couldn't love the Indians and I wouldn't give up because I believed God had called me to give them the Gospel.

The only blow that could crush the spirit within me had fallen! I was entirely bereft.

Sob followed sob and the climax of misery was reached when I felt Domot's warm tears falling down on my cheek and neck.

A convulsion seized me. Then wonder of wonders! Into my heart there crept gently, silently, sweetly, a perfect calm.

Tears ceased, a big sigh escaped and love was born. A love for the Indians not my own.

> " Were the whole realm of nature mine
> That were a present far too small.
> Love so amazing, so divine
> Demands my soul, my life, my all."

November 16th. Saddle Mountain. The big gospel tent (16 x 30 feet, bought with the surplus money from the camp-meeting, June 27th–July 1st, plus pelt money, plus bead work money, $46.63) went up to-day.

November 20th. Fire! Fire! Fire! Great clouds of smoke rolling overhead all day.

November 21st. Fire! Fire! Fire! The prairie and mountains are all ablaze. We were out all night fighting the flames.

November 22d. The danger is past and the whole landscape a charred scene of desolation.

December 3d. Last night I had a very vivid dream. I thought I was wakened from sleep by the most terrific explosion.

The whole earth seemed to be breaking up. Saddle Mountain and all the little hills were thrown over and over and the creek was hurled into the sky.

Crash followed crash and thunder and lightning added horror to the scene.

I held my breath in terrible affright, expecting the earth under me to upheave at any moment. I tried to recall some promise to which I might cling when the end came, but the confusion and turmoil drove everything from my mind.

The shame that filled my heart upon not being able to recall a single promise was almost insufferable.

At last a fearful explosion took place and I felt myself sinking, sinking, sinking. My senses dulled, the commotion subsided, the tumbling mountains vanished and Jesus Himself stood beside me saying, " Daughter, be of good cheer, I have overcome the world." Then it was that I realized more fully than ever before that I was trusting in *Jesus Himself* rather than in His promises.

I woke with a mind full of perfect peace, glad that I was still in the house of the interpreter with work to do on my way to the Celestial City.

FOUR SCENES

I

In an upper room, in a Canadian city, a tired mother lies down to rest surrounded by every luxury earth could bestow. For more than threescore years and ten she has fought the battles of life, and now the battle with death is drawing near. Her strength is well-nigh spent, and when the final conflict comes, makes no resistance, but goes an easy prey, and the king of terrors smiles as he stoops to claim his own.

But his own is only the cold and lifeless form, for the spirit has escaped his iron clutch. *Death swallowed up in victory !*

II

An Indian sat listening to an earnest talk on the necessity of Christians making all haste to rescue their friends from the eternal burning. His heart was stirred, and next evening said to the missionary : " Last night your talk made me afraid, and I thought a long time after I laid down to sleep. My father and mother never

heard about the Jesus road. They were good
Indians, kind to everybody and never got mad
and fought. Every day, every day, every day
they were the same. If they had heard about
the Jesus road they would have caught it in a
hurry, for they were wise. They are lost now
but I have been praying the Great Father to
look for them and save them, for they were too
good to be burned up. My heart cried when I
prayed, so maybe He will hear me."

Victory swallowed up in death!

III

All day clouds of smoke from distant prairie
fires had been driven hither and thither by the
wind.

The Indians camping along Saddle Mountain
Creek were undisturbed and as the shadows fell,
crept into their tepees to wrap the draperies
of their couches about them and lie down to
pleasant dreams.

Darkness in full maturity had settled on the
earth and the voices of nature were stilled.
Night was far advanced, when fitful flashes of
light began to streak the sky, and soon the
mountains round about were a solid wall of fire.

Flames leaped higher and higher as the
breezes blew, trees crackled and fell, the grass
became a living wall of red! Saddle Mountain
is burning! Saddle Mountain is burning! And

the flames tossed and twisted and rolled about each other as they flew upward, and then curled and tumbled down over the valley.

Horses fled as if crazed as the fire singed their legs, cows galloped past, gophers darted here and there in terrible affright, dogs barked. Wreaths of hot smoke rose higher and higher and whirlwinds of cinders were scattered to the gale.

Daylight had come but with it no decrease in the threatening element. Fire! fire! fire! Smoke! smoke! smoke! And the roaring of it was heard afar off, even at Rainy Mountain. Where are the missionaries? Are they safe in the house of the interpreter, or have they escaped to the storm cellar to pray to the God of Heaven to send rain or a fire-engine to save the poor Indians from destruction?

Long before the first ray of sunlight vied with the surrounding blaze they were up and dressed, pushing their way through the standing corn-stalks, underbrush and shrubs, armed with garments snatched from the missionary barrels and plunged in water.

On they went till something attracted their attention. Then they paused and wondered. An Indian with a firebrand in his hand raced from place to place starting a whole row of little fires half a mile beyond. Lucius, their interpreter, is at work. *And the wind is in his favor!*

The fires unite as they are carried rapidly towards the great conflagration and the missionaries clap down the flames at the outer edge while the interpreter is busy at the front.

Eyes are blinded by the smoke, throats are parched, hair, eyebrows and eyelashes are scorched, yet there is no thought of either failure or retreat. On comes the roaring, raging, flaming fiend with power and might, threatening destruction to everybody and everything in its path. *But the winds are contrary.*

On comes the little fire kindled by the Indian, lacking in strength and magnitude. *And the winds are favorable.*

The two enemies draw nearer and nearer. The space between them grows smaller and smaller till with one wild leap the mighty volume bears down upon the weaker and "Clouds began to darken all the hill and smoke to roll in dusty wreaths!"

The battle's ended, *and death is swallowed up in victory!*

IV

The earth was full of wickedness. Sin was triumphing on every side. The chosen people were in captivity, and man was a failure from first to last.

Jesus of Nazareth came and went, "despised and rejected of men." Others followed in His footsteps, leaving behind a few struggling Christians formed into a church to combat against a world wholly given over to idolatry and vileness in every form.

With the Holy Spirit's influence on through the centuries they have come gathering new strength along the way, Peter and Paul along the lines in the front, and Mary and Martha behind.

To meet them Satan has brought forth monster evils, enough to close the conflict in one speedy onset could he but bring about the hour. But this is not permitted. *The Holy Spirit breathes against.* Nearer and nearer the opposing forces are drawing, and in God's own time the dreaded moment will come when earth and hell and all the powers of darkness shall be vanquished before the army of the Lord. *And death shall be forever swallowed up in victory!* Soldiers of Jesus Christ, in the army of the Lord! In God's name wake up!

The battle is raging. The war is on, and millions are already lost who might have been saved.

One mother calls back to earth : " O grave, where is thy victory ? " Another wails out : " O death, here is thy sting! " and the message of peace was sent to both.

To see the mountains, trees and plains one wild hurricane of fire is terrible in the extreme, but what must it be when not only the outside of the earth but the earth itself shall melt with fervid heat?

Awake! awake! put on thy strength, O Zion!

Move forward! move forward all along the line! And fight till the last sun sinks and "Victory! Victory! Victory! The Lord God Omnipotent reigneth!" vibrates from pole to pole. "*And there shall be no more death.*"

March 15, 1898. Poor old Soldate died to-day.

The ropes had been arranged under her and as soon as the breath was out of the body they corded the quilts around her, and sagging till it scraped the ground, the human bundle was hurried from the tepee and galloped to the grave.

In her hands she clasped a roll of "Jesus patchwork" that had carried a message of love from a white sister. Who shall say that it did not carry the message of life?

May 10th. While the air is full of "wars and rumors of wars" and letters are pouring in asking: "Are the missionaries safe?" "Don't you think you had better come home?" "You are dear brave girls not to be afraid," etc., etc., an organization was formed to-day that breathes of peace. It isn't a church and it isn't a woman's mission circle exactly.

Our nearest Baptist church is seventeen miles

away. It is into this church that all converts in our district are baptized.

After prayerful and careful consideration we decided that it would be better to retain our membership at Rainy Mountain instead of forming a new organization.

Therefore we wrote to Chicago and asked if the Woman's Baptist Home Mission Society would recognize a mission circle composed of men as well as women.

The matter was brought before the Board and we were informed that there was no reason in the world why men as well as women might not belong to the circles *especially if they paid their dues.*

All morning we sewed on quilt-tops and after dinner the new road was explained.

"Before Jesus went away He asked all who loved Him to spread the good news everywhere.

Little churches were formed and many meetings were held on the sly. The devil was mad and killed many of the first Christians. Men went out two by two to carry the news and walked till they were tired. The women did what they could and all prayed and prayed and prayed.

Men work at big things and when they stop they sit down. Women work at many little things. Their work is never done.

Their work for Jesus is different also. Men

organize churches and become pastors. Women
organize little mission circles in these churches
and meet to pray, study, pack barrels, give and
push. They do all this to obey Jesus' last command. Once a beautiful young woman came to
the Training School and said : ' I feel that Jesus
wants me to go to the poor Indians, the kind
that wear blankets, feathers and paint.'

Her name was Miss Reeside.

The Woman's Baptist Home Mission Society
is the name of the organization composed of all
the little mission circles in our churches that sent
her to the Kiowas.

To-day we are going to stand with those
praying women, organize a circle and give money
to send the Gospel to another tribe.

We will give money also for a church but
giving the Gospel to others is away ahead."

The climax was reached when Miss McLean
told of " Baby-Band." Could it be possible that
their babies could give money to Jesus too?

Before the talks were finished Boton in gorgeous apparel and face outrivaling the " yellow leaves in autumn " signed : " Give me a
money barrel. I want to put fifty cents in right
now."

Kokom arose, Popebah arose, Montahahty
arose, with a baby on her back and coming to
the front, followed by all their children and grand-
children, halted. Money barrels for each were

taken and then the man facing the sea of earnest upturned faces said :

" We never heard anything like this before. We thought we just gave our hearts to Jesus, cut off our bad roads and walked as straight as we could up, up, up to the Beautiful Home.

We never knew before that we could give money to Jesus. We have heard great news to-day. Now I am ready to be baptized and I will give money to Jesus for my children and grand-children as long as I live. I have spoken."

Turning and looking down into our faces he signed :

" Isn't it kind of Jesus to *let the poor Indians give to send His Gospel to somebody else !* "

The organization was formed in New Testament and Indian fashion. " With one consent " and by a showing of hearts, rather than of a showing of hands.

May 31st. The officers of the society were not chosen May 10th. Their hearts were too full that day with thoughts of Jesus' kindness in letting them give money to send His Gospel to others to bring them down to thinking about them-selves.

To-day they were selected with a care that was astonishing. No one was elected who danced, played cards or walked the least bit crooked. They were men and women of *recognized spiri-*

tuality who walked "like on a hill" where all saw that they had no crazy roads.

President,	-	-	-	Popebah.
Vice-President,		-	-	Big Red.
Treasurer,	-	-	-	Ananthy.
Secretary,	-	-	-	Lucius.

Each was called upon to make a talk. Popebah with the perspiration standing out on her face in great beads said :

"Because this is my first president I don't know what to say—I don't know what to do—but I will say what I think.

I am the head officer and I want you to do what I tell you. We are a little branch of a big tree (W. B. H. M. S.), and we must all try to stay on, grow and get strong. I want you all to work together for Jesus and then we can do something. That's all."

Lucius, the secretary :

"When Indians kill a beef and spend ten or fifteen dollars for groceries and pray to Jesus He doesn't like it for He doesn't get anything. If any of you Christians want to have a prayer-meeting in your houses tell us and we will all come and bring our own food and then you can give five cents or one dollar to the society to send the Gospel to somebody else.

Jesus will like this better than if you eat it all up yourselves."

"What shall we call our missionary society? What name shall we give it?" After much discussion the decision was given as follows:

"Because we are Kiowa Indians and live near Saddle Mountain and a lot of us have found the Jesus road and want the other tribes to find it we would like to be like God's light upon the mountain—Daw-kee-boom-gee-k'oop."

July 11th. Returning on Friday from a food trip to Fort Sill we found that great preparations had been made about a mile away for a "Missionary Big Eat" on *Sunday.* We told them Jesus would have liked it better if they had planned it for another day, but as they had "made-the-road" and invited the people we would go and give the Jesus talk.

The beef was killed on Saturday and tables and chairs gathered up from every place.

After the regular Sunday morning "Jesus talk" Ananthy came forward and said: "When I was sick last winter I told Jesus if He would make me well I would kill a beef and call in all the Christians. The missionaries think it is like the Ghost-Dance road, but it is not. Jesus made me better and I had the meeting here to-day to thank Him and to give ten cents apiece for each of my children, for my husband, my son-in-law and my grandchildren. I want the money sent to the society that sends the Gospel to other tribes."

The husband arose, his face in dead earnest, and said: "My wife is a Christian and some of my children but I have been waiting for my eldest daughter. I wait no longer. I believe the Holy Spirit has touched my heart and I am converted straight. I have spoken."

July 19th. "Dan-kee-boom-gee-k'oop" had its first full fledged missionary meeting to-day. The arbor was crowded and little red money barrels were in evidence everywhere.

The talk was on the great Commission. "Jesus commanded us to spread the good news. He said nothing about building churches. He put heads on all people and brains (or sense) in some of them and knew we would think that out for ourselves. He just said, 'Go into all the world and preach the Gospel to every creature and I will be with you.'

He wants us to hurry too, for He did not say one—two—three—go. He just said 'Go!' and that means that we are to start right off as soon as we are converted.

To-day we are going to put money in two china barrels, one for our church and the other to send the Gospel. The gospel barrel is 'away ahead.'"

Up they came with faces beaming, babies

crowing and dogs barking. Such a crush!
Cheerful givers? Why, I never saw any cheerful givers before. Laughing and crying they
poured their money into both barrels.

Ananthy, the treasurer, broke them open with
a big stone and there were $17.26 to send the
Gospel to others, and $17.34 for the church—
eight cents too much on the wrong side, but it
was a glorious showing—$34.60. (Total build-
ing fund, $19.54.)

Boton arose: "I am going to give a Big-mis-
sionary-thank-you-to-Jesus-eat at my camp next
Sunday. I invite you all to come."

"Boton, are you giving this 'Big Eat' to
please Jesus or yourself, which?" I asked.

"To please Jesus."

"Then He would like you to have it on another day."

A pause followed.

"I will have it on Saturday, the nearest day
to Jesus day," he said.

July 24th. One hundred and seventy responded to the invitation. No race on earth
can compete with the North American Indian
in the artistic splendor of his native costume.

Boton greeted us in magnificent array, yellow
beaded buckskins, hair wrapped in strips of
beaver and his face painted the brightest tints of
red and yellow.

His two wives dressed in their worst, sat on a cow skin with piles and piles of raw beef, cooking as fast as the fire could cook it.

The table, spread with canvas, oilcloth and gay blankets, was surrounded by tents, tepees, covered wagons, saddle horses and dogs.

A gospel talk, in which the "two-money-roads" were explained, was given just as if it had been Sunday. The dinner followed. At the close of the afternoon service Boton arose in his gorgeous attire and said :

"The Great Father loves everybody. I have called you all to this 'Big Eat' that you may be pleased with Him. A son and a daughter will give money to Jesus to-day to send the Gospel to another tribe. When they grow up I do not want them to walk away from this good road."

Was it a vision or was it a dream? There arose from the ground and came bashfully forward a little Indian maiden about six years of age. She was gowned in yellow buckskin with moccasins exquisitely beaded, and on each cheek a round red spot was painted. Her coal black hair fell in soft waves about her shoulders, giving to her face an artistic finish that brought out the perfection of its outline.

Standing a moment as if conscious of her beauty she lifted one hand and from between its ring-covered fingers there dropped into the treasury of the Lord a fifty cent piece.

The baby boy was then carried up and from his chubby hand there fell another fifty cent piece. The giving to the Jesus road was theirs. The ceremony was over.

At the back end of the arbor a sick man lay on a cot. When the children were through giving he staggered to his feet and managed to get up to the front. He would not sit down, but leaning over the back of a chair said: "It is hard for Indians to get money. I am a great sufferer but I don't say anything. You are a woman and can read the Bible. If you had no Bible we would not listen to you.

It is no use to collect this money. There isn't going to be a church at Saddle Mountain. We don't want one. That is what we all say. I don't want to have anything to do with that missionary society. They want to steal our money from us. I have fifty cents here. If I could put it in Jesus' own hand I would be glad, but I cannot, so I put in the barrel for the church. If it is built we will see it with our two eyes."

(Total building fund, $20.04.)

July 31st, Sunday. After Ananthy, treasurer of Daw-kee-boom-gee-k'oop, had handed in the missionary money ($17.26) in a beautiful beaded bag to be taken to Chicago, Lucius arose and said:

"Yesterday I went to the school to see my

children and I got them all over into the farmer's house. I opened the Bible and read to them about that big feller who came to Jesus at night and couldn't understand how he could be babied again.

Jesus explained to him very plain that it was the spirit that had to be babied.

After I had read the Bible I made a talk to my children and told them they were like big stones pressing on my heart till they found Jesus and then they fell off. There was no stone on for Amos because he was saved. If I could save them myself I would do it fast but only Jesus could do that through His Holy Spirit and I wanted them all to kneel down and I would ask Jesus to send the Holy Spirit into their hearts just as soon as they had sense enough to believe.

Then I knelt down with my little family and prayed till the tears dropped on the floor. When we got up my little Jessie walked half-way to her seat and then turned around and came back and stood by my chair. 'Father,' she said, 'I believe I have given my heart to Jesus. I believe He has saved me and as soon as I have an opportunity I want to be baptized.'

When I heard my little daughter say these words the stone fell off my heart and tears came out on my face, for I knew the Great Father had answered my prayer.

Take this dollar with you to the Jesus woman's

society as a thank-you to Jesus and tell them to hurry and send the Gospel to another tribe.

Tell the white people if they talk and pray with their children they will give their hearts to Jesus as soon as they have sense enough to believe and then when they grow up they won't go into crazy-swopping-houses (saloons) and pick up bad roads.

I believe my other children will find Jesus as soon as they get sense enough to understand."

August 1st. Vacation.

The calamity of the year has been the retirement of Miss Marietta J. Reeside from the work at Rainy Mountain. As long as the Kiowa tribe survives, her name and Miss Ballew's will live in the hearts of the people.

August 11th. Such a time as I have had getting to the railroad. It rained and all the creeks and rivers were up.

One town we passed through was in an excitement over the capture of Red Buck, a noted outlaw. He was brought in shot, roped to a board and photographed.

Building fund, $18.94 (the original $1.10 retained).

IV

*Giving the Land to Jesus—Oh, for a Man !—
The Den—Two Quarters*

SEPTEMBER 28, 1898. For over a year Miss McLean and I had been closely related in the work. Almost as closely as the Siamese Twins. Our one room was just large enough for the bed, the cook-stove, a little table and three chairs. In it we washed, ironed, cooked, mopped, cleaned and wrote from twenty-five to two hundred letters a month, with the Indians constantly coming in to " heap see."

On the wall at one side of the stove Miss McLean made such a pretty little medicine cabinet. On the other side I had my book-shelf and spool cabinet desk. Then there was a closet in which we could hang up everything except ourselves, and there were times when we wished we could do that.

While working at Elk Creek I had received a letter from Mrs. H. Stevens of Dayton, Ohio, stating that "she felt called of God to invest $300 towards making me more comfortable, that my life might be prolonged to do more and better work for the Master."

She wrote : " If you build a house I would like

you to own the land it is on ; let it be yours entirely to be disposed of any time you think best
and the money reinvested to make yourself comfortable in any way and in any place you choose.
You are to use the money for your *comfort* and
your comfort only until you are worth $10,000 or
until death.

I solemnly enjoin upon you to use the money
in the best way you know how to add to your
comfort. You will certainly break my last will
and testament if you do not."

Talking the matter over with Lucius it was decided that I might build a small one-roomed
house on his land.

October 4th. Just as Miss McLean and I were
going to pile into a lumber wagon to go off to
fix an Indian house some one came out and
signed to me : "You better cut off going."

Numbers of Indians were gathering under the
arbor and it suddenly flashed across my mind
that they were going to formally forbid the
building of the den, for I knew there had been a
lot of kicking and talking going on about the
building all over the reservation.

Some Indians had said : " Yes, we understand.
First the Jesus woman come and sit down in Indian houses, then they build houses for themselves and churches and pretty soon a Jesus man
comes and puts up a fence and Indians are cut

off. Miss Crawford was sent to Elk Creek. Why didn't she stay there?

What did she go to Saddle Mountain for? She is getting ahead, getting ahead, getting ahead and after a while a Jesus man will come and put up a fence. Tell her to go back to Elk Creek and sit down in the house that was built for her."

Trying to smile and look cheerful I went to the arbor and seated myself beside the interpreter as usual. "You can't sit there," they signed. "You are to sit out in the middle and you are not to laugh for it is to be a very wonderful council."

A thing like a butcher's block was wheeled into the centre and I meekly walked over and sat on it.

"Tell us what you want," came next and turning to Lucius I said, " Oh, Lucius, we must talk to Jesus first."

Down upon our knees we went and I think I dictated to the Almighty for I remember telling Him if He didn't give me the room I'd have to go home.

The prayer over I made my talk:

" Five years ago I came to the Kiowa Indians to tell you about Jesus. First I went to Elk Creek but there were so few Indians there that the Holy Spirit told me to go out and hunt for more.

Domot, the oldest man in this council, came to Elk Creek and invited me to come to Saddle Mountain. I came and you all know how I have lived among you, asking for nothing except your protection. I lived in a tent and in a tepee till Lucius asked me to his home. Then he bought the lumber and I paid the carpenter and we built another room. It belongs to Lucius and not to me.

The gospel tent also belongs to the Kiowas and if I go away I cannot take it with me. It is yours. You all know, for I have told you, that I will never ask for any land for Jesus.

That is your business, not mine.

It may be a long long time before a Jesus House can be built and what I want you to let me do is to build a small house on Lucius' land to be moved off when the church is up. My head is tired all the time and at night I jump and turn like a fish when it is pulled out of the water.

I did not mean to hide anything when I spoke only to Lucius. That is the white man's road, but the Kiowa road is different.

To-day I ask you all to make a wise road for me."

For two solid hours I sat on that old butcher's block and only once did I get any information.

"The road is dangerous; it is like coming against rocks," one man signed.

Domot's cigarette papers blew away and I

ran after them to get a chance to cry for I was
horribly unstrung.

"My child, do take care of yourself. You
know your father shortened his usefulness by
overwork and you owe it to your Maker to take
care of the wonderful health He has given to
you." These words were in one of my mother's
last letters and I could not help thinking of them
then at this time.

At last the council was over and I was asked
to listen to talks from the representative men of
Saddle Mountain.

Domot: "I am the oldest man here and I
will make my talk first (mark the etiquette—
oldest man first). The Indians who are not
walking in the Jesus road are very mad, but I
am not afraid of them. You left Elk Creek and
came here and you have been kind to us and to
our children.

I am not a Christian but I have been thinking wisely. You have helped us and white
friends have helped us, sending us dresses,
patchwork, some coat and some pant. The
Ghost-Dance chiefs who are making all the
trouble do not help anybody, for they try to
pull us all back. This is true.

Now we have talked it all over very carefully and this is what we think:

You may build your house on Lucius' land.
After a while white men are going to come in

here and cut up the land and take all that is over. They are dangerous.

We must hurry up and look for land for Jesus and put His brand on it and when He comes and finds His brand He will know that we did not forget Him.

Then when the Jesus House is built you can move yours over to it with no trouble. This is what we think and it is a wise road. I have spoken."

"There is just one thing that gives us trouble," said another. "The Ghost-Dance people are kicking and abusing Lucius very strongly because he is willing to let this house be built on his land. This is what we think. We will let their talk hit us like the wind. We don't fight the wind or look at it; it hits us and passes over and pretty soon it is gone and we are not hurt."

When the talks were all over Domot again spoke :

"White men are dangerous ; they are smart and sly. Maybe so after us old men pass away they will come in here and drive our children out of the Jesus House and worship the Great Spirit in it themselves. We want you to get paper and ink and draw up a road that will make this an Indian church forever."

"I'll make it tighter than that," I replied. "I'll make it an Indian 'Big-water' Church forever and if your children pick up the 'Little-water-road' they will not be able to carry the church off with them."

Some kind of a paper was then drawn up and one by one these "mighty men of valor" came forward and taking the pen, held it up to Jesus asking Him with tears streaming down their faces to accept their land and hold it tight from the white men, for their children, that they might have a Jesus House to worship in when they themselves had passed away.

Their talks, the dignity of the whole proceedings, the simplicity and directness of the ceremony, the perfect order and decorum and the honest desire to do something to please Jesus and do it right so overwhelmed me that all I could do at the end was to sign to Lucius :

"Pray and thank Jesus for putting this wonderful road in your heart."

Before the council broke up my scattered senses returned and I made one more talk.

"There are two things I want to say. First: If you give Jesus land with no water on it it will look as if the 'Little-water-road' was yours. Look for land with water on it.

Second: We are two Jesus women and we cannot sit down away off on the prairie alone. Look for land near you. I have spoken."

"All right good. Now you can tell the white friends we are ready for the church."

" Why should we ask the white friends to work from sunrise to sunset to build a church for you while you sit waiting?" I signed. "It is a crazy road. I will not walk on it. We will teach you how to build a Jesus House for yourselves."

Consternation was written on every face and the council broke up.

If we are taught " to give till it pinches " surely the Lord means us to pinch these people till they give and I mean to, good and hard. It is my private opinion gleaned from bitter experience in the wild and woolly West that it would be a great deal better if fewer churches were built and more money spent in making the heroic pastors and their families at least comfortable.

Jesus died to save sinners and sometimes I am tempted to believe that some sinners think the missionaries should do about everything else for them.

The great Commission does not say that we are to teach the people to observe *us* do all things, but we are to teach them to do all things themselves.

October 5th. Domot appeared early.

" I want to give you a wise talk," he signed.

" We have all talked it over and we think your road is not good.

Indians are poor. They cannot build their own small houses. Government helps us.

We cannot build a Jesus House. When we
are hungry and tired we won't try."

I replied :

" All the men and women over here who are
truly converted will try and Jesus will help them.
If any will not try they must look for the Jesus
road again, for they have missed it. Jesus makes
His spiritual children willing to do hard things
for Him.

I cannot ask for money for your church."

October 6th. Two of the council men called.

" Last night we had another council," they
signed, " and this is what we think. Two Jesus
women to sit down with us is good ; we will look
for land near."

November 16th. For several days an old yellow abandoned sick dog had been hanging
around the house and yesterday before the Indians started to issue we asked Lucius to give it
a military funeral. He went to the creek, fired
and drove away.

This morning the dog came to the door with
part of his head blown off, one eye gone and the
other red and blood-shot.

What was to be done ?

Neither of us could kill him. Oh, for a man !
(It was the first time in all my life that that intense yearning had entered my heart !)

Acting as a substitute we mixed up a box of

"rough-on-rats" with all the scraps we could find. The poor creature fairly gobbled everything and then went off on a joyful trot.

About noon my conscience began to work. I found him lying behind the wood-pile shivering and shaking all over.

He knew me at once and began wagging his tail in thankfulness for the "Big Eat." Going back to the house for a pan of water and a kindergarten chair I sat beside him till the end came. All that loving hands could do was done for him and he knew me till the last. Fastening his one eye upon me the tail wagged slower and slower and slower, the eye got setter and setter and setter and when the tail went down to rise no more I knew "the poor doggie was dead." Did I cry? Didn't I? Hypocrites ought to and repent before it is too late.

December 17th. Have just returned from a trip for food and we had a picnic.

It rained and blew and stormed but the horse and mule and lumber wagon are back with twenty-four pounds of fresh ham, fifteen dozen eggs, twenty-five pounds of corn-meal, thirty pounds of butter, a stick of sausage, thirty-five live quails, a pig's liver and some condensed missionary.

December 28th. Christmas with its whirl of preparations is over. Jesus got the best present on the tree, $31.18. (To sending the Gospel to others, $11.93. To building fund, $19.25.)

December 29th. Just as the sun peeped above the eastern horizon poor old Stumbling Bear hobbled from his tepee and with hands held towards the sun and the heavens (the attitude of worship) called so all the sleeping camp could hear :

"Thank you, Jesus ! Thank you, Jesus ! Thank you, Jesus ! The Jesus women have been kind to us ; we are poor and sick and they have made our hearts glad ! Thank you, Jesus, for all the Jesus women everywhere."

Then he crept back and seated himself between his blind wife and dying son.

January 6, 1899. Early this morning they came for us to see Gah-yi-day die. For several days we had been carrying him food, etc., and up to the last he said Jesus was in his heart. His two wives sat beside him on the bed. When the end came they rivaled each other in screaming and in demonstrations of affection.

"I loved him ! I loved him ! I loved him !" signed one. " My heart burns me like fire. My husband is dead, *my* husband ! The other woman loved him not."

Lifting the lifeless hand to her lips and slipping the limp arm about her neck the wife contented herself in holding possession,

The rude coffin was brought in, the body was placed in it wrapped in a brilliant blanket of red, Miss McLean nailed down the cover and in less than two hours from the death the poor man was buried beneath the sod. It was he who once wanted to put fifty cents in Jesus' own hand.

January 19th. As I struck the first match in the little den the door swung silently open and an Indian stood before me.

"I cannot sit down," he signed. "I must hurry back. I came to tell you that on Saturday Jesus came into my heart. I will be baptized when the grass grows."

How my heart throbbed as the door closed!

February 20th, Sunday. "Come here," said Paudlekeah, as we entered the tent. Taking me by the hand he led me to the picture roll and pointing to a horrible idol signed: "Why? Why? Why do the people across the big water put such ugly faces on the gods they prayed to? Why don't they make good faces?"

Turning the picture over till he found "The Triumphal Entry" he signed again:

"Why? Why? Why did the white men give Jesus that nasty little mule to ride on? Why didn't they give Him a big war-horse?"

When he learned that the little mule had never been broken and did not throw Jesus he signed:

" The little mule had more sense than the white men chiefs."

February 24th. " Come with me," said Kokom. " A woman hen is sick in bed and won't get up. When I give her ' chuck ' she bites and turns her head away."

It was Miss McLean who diagnosed the case. Mrs. Hen simply wanted to set.

March 24th. Little Annie Kokom was buried to-day with all her belongings and the bedstead was placed on her grave.

March 27th. It snowed in the night and turned bitter cold. Thinking of the stricken family I took two warm quilts and went off in search of it.

There was consternation in the camp when I arrived. "You have walked on a dangerous road," they signed. " We have put all our cattle in the corral. The wolves are hungry and chased some of us on horseback. They have eaten our calves. They would have catched you if they had seen you.

You cannot hear. They are howling up on Saddle Mountain and all around. We will take you back with our horses. We will not let you walk."

I found Popebah lying on a mattress on the floor in the house. She signed: " I have been sick and weak since my trouble. I am glad you came to see me before you go away.

My little daughter owned this purse and after Jesus took her I opened it and found these two quarters.

Since I have been lying here I have studied in my heart to find out how Jesus would like the money spent. I thought very truly and I would like you to take it with you and give it to the Jesus Woman Society and tell them to hurry and send the good news to others."

April 17th. Vacation.
Building fund, $38.19.

V

*The Going of Miss McLean—An Indian Recep-
tion—Testimonies—The Coming of Miss Bare
—Self-Support—Payment—Confessing Their
Faults—A Birthday Party—The Association*

AUGUST 22, 1899. Back to work! (with thirty dollars' worth of calico at two and a half cents a yard for the quilts, checked on my ticket).

Some changes have taken place. Miss Mc-Lean has been transferred to Rainy Mountain and Lucius has given up his position as government farmer to come back home and interpret for Jesus for about half the pay.

September 1st. It was Papadone who gave the welcome "Big Eat." There were one hundred and twenty-five guests without counting the dogs, cows, horses and dead-heads that surrounded the arbor.

I think a whole cow was demolished besides no end of canned stuff, candies and fruit, and then the host led in the speech-making.

"I am a Christian man and I wanted to do something to please Jesus for bringing her back so I asked you all here to-day.

When Jesus gives me any money I always

put by five cents for Him. I understand He likes the money we work for best so I have kept some for Him. My wife and I have saved $4.50. We want half of it to go to the church and half to send the Gospel to another tribe.

Jesus is the man who gives us all our money. We ought to give some cents to Him."

A tall woman with a sad, beautiful face arose. She was dressed in faded garments and wore the Indian mourning overdress. In her hand she held a little red money barrel and opening it said: "I am a poor woman but Jesus is my Saviour. My brothers and sisters, I stand before you not to surprise you by coming to a Big Eat so soon after my husband's death, but because I feel my heart true to Jesus.

He gave us these money barrels and I have come with twenty cents in mine, because I do not want to keep it back or open it empty before Him."

A little girl came up with seventy cents, a man with one dollar and then they were ready for the Jesus talk.

Lucius made this statement at the close:

"You all know I used to be government farmer and whatever the agent told me to do I did it. I am farmer for Jesus now and I am going to sow His seed all over you. If you open your hearts the seed will go in and grow.

I am going to give Jesus all my time. Don't

kick or abuse us when we come to see you but listen to what we say for we want to help you.

When any trouble comes to us let us think it over carefully, ask Jesus for help and then pull through with all our strength."

Prayers followed. Earnest prayers for the children returning to school in the morning that they might learn to read and come back to read the Jesus-Book to them.

September 3d, Sunday. Gave an earnest talk on the work of the Holy Spirit to-day. " In order to have Him work through us we must clean everything that hinders out of the way and then let Him use us. We are like water pails. The Great Father keeps filling us with living water and the Holy Spirit tells us where to carry it.

Bad roads not cut off are like mud in the bottom of the pail and the unconverted won't drink."

Mokeen was on his feet as soon as the lesson was over.

" It is all true what she says," he said. " Some of you carry the old roads in the bottom of your pails and we all know it.

Empty out the mud and let Jesus pour in clean fresh waters and the sinners will drink."

Some one called out:

" Mokeen ! Why don't you drink the living

water yourself? It is true some of us put mud in it, but you know where the good water is. Why don't you drink?

The tears run down your son Lucius' face when he talks about you. You should come to Jesus and let Him save you."

"The devil tempted Jesus after He was baptized," said Kokom. "He did not fall down because He was the Son of God. I am only a human man.

I have just been to church four times in four months. I am like a bird up in the sky that comes down to drink.

To-day I have come to the Jesus House and have taken a good long drink of sweet living water and feel better."

Ah-mot-ah-ah: "I am forty-five years old and have followed every crossroad I came to.

First I heard about Sunday, then about the Bible and now I have found out that the Great Father loves me. When I heard that He gave His Son to save me I was ashamed of myself and said: 'Here, take me as I am and save me.' I have come here glad to-day."

Keapetate: "Sometimes I get mad and my friends say: 'You are half devil and half Christian,' but I understand if we go wrong and ask Jesus to forgive us He will do it. My husband says mean things to me sometimes. Once he said, 'The devil is your husband.' I said to him : 'If the devil is my husband who are you ? I am a Christian and only want one husband.' Once I got up to talk for Jesus at another place and the Jesus man sang to make me stop talking. It was the devil that told him to sing so I talked on for Jesus and beat them both."

Dangerous Bear : " What I know I will confess. Sometimes I quarrel with my wife but I don't want it to last all day. I always forgive in about an hour. My wife is kind and don't want to quarrel with me but I always start it. Remember me in your prayers. This fifty-five cents is my little daughter's last Jesus money. She sits down with Jesus now."

" This earth belongs to Jesus," said Heenkey, " and we are here to work it for Him. He gives us everything to work with and if we don't go ahead we are lazy. If a man not a Christian goes past my place and sees it not growing he will go round and say : ' Look at Heenkey. He is a Christian. He don't do nothing and all the Great Father has given him is wasted.'

We must do something for Jesus. If a cow has a calf and keeps on having one every year, after a while she will have a whole lot. It is the same with us. If we do a little for Jesus every year after a while we will have something to give to Him. Every morning I think out my work for the day. After I know it I tell Jesus about it and then ask Him to plan my spiritual work for me for I can't do that.   Then I go ahead the best way I know how.   If Jesus sends spiritual work I quit my own right off and do His first."

October 11th.   She hopped off the train like a robin and we all knew that the new missionary, Miss K. E. Bare, would fill the bill to a T.   After camping round holding meetings every day and night till the 17th we returned to Saddle Mountain soused to the skin.

October 22d.   The meetings were held in the den all day.   It is only 13 x 13 feet yet forty Indians packed themselves in like sardines in a box with rain and mud for liquid.   The " Bear-woman " had room enough to open her two eyes.

December 3d.   Reports have reached us that the Reservation is to be opened soon and the Indians are running everywhere gathering up the bones of their dead and bringing them to the different missions.   Living or dead it seems as if they must " move on."

Kokom came in to-day with the bones of his two sons.   " How nice it will be," said the mother, " to have my boys over here and when my turn comes I will lie down beside them,   My heart is glad,"

December 17th. It was midnight. The yard was full of screaming and Miss Bare came over and wakened me. Spotted Horse had galloped his team twenty-five miles while his wife held in her arms the lifeless body of their first and only child. A missionary box was prepared. The little one was placed in it and carried into the den. After much persuasion the mother finally laid down in my cot and the father threw himself wrapped in a blanket on the floor.

Leaving them alone with their dead I slipped over to the other room and got into bed with Miss Bare. We were up early. The baby was safe but the father and mother were gone.

On the mountains on one side of the graveyard we distinguished the father. On the mountains on the other side the mother. One screamed and the other responded till the whole valley echoed and reëchoed with grief. It was noon before the grave was finished, the freezing cold adding to the painfulness of the situation. Descending from the mountains the father and mother crept nearer and nearer. Reaching the fence lines they threw themselves down on their faces and shriek followed shriek. Running to the help of the mother she thrust a photograph of herself and babe into my hand, clinging to something else under her blanket. It was a little Mexican puppy, the playmate of her child, and when it was killed and put in the grave, followed by the screaming father, we took the poor mother back to the house.

December 25th. It was the saddest of Christmases. Everybody cried and shrieked. No sooner would one outburst subside than another wagon would drive up and demonstrations burst out afresh.

After dinner four money barrels were placed on a piece of rag carpet on the ground. We had only had three before ; one for sending the Gospel to others, one for the church and one for the Baby Band. It was now time to introduce *self-support.* The fourth barrel was for the Interpreter's salary. When it was explained Lucius said : " I don't like the road. I would sooner earn my living another way. It makes me feel 'shamed."

Replying I said, " Some white women take in washing to help pay our salaries, Lucius. It is not my way or your way but His. He wants us to take care of ourselves over here, as soon as ever we can, that the money that now comes may be used in sending other missionaries to other tribes."

One by one they came forward, some brown hands parting with their last coin. " Because this tent is getting old and will soon tear down I am going to give all the cents I have to the church," said a poor modern Christian. Yet three years ago this same man was white with rage because it was hinted that some time there might be a Jesus House at Saddle Mountain. Every hand in the tent was raised for prayers, saved and unsaved, and with bowed heads we again gave to Jesus the best present on the tree.

To sending the Gospel, $10.15. Church building, $18.46. Baby Band, $10.10. Interpreter's salary, $9.70. Total, $48.41.

February 14, 1900. Payment! On for Rainy Mountain! Our Indians camp by themselves and a big flag marks the soldiers-for-Jesus-camp. All day long they tie quilts (having made the tops at their homes), buy and sell. Every night they talk and sing for Jesus. "We work and pray to beat the devil," as they say.

Domot found us at the school and after shaking hands signed: "I have sold a horse and want to give Jesus three dollars for His church." Bowing his head he prayed, adjusted his blanket and was gone. Dignity, reverence, generosity and businesslike manliness with honesty. What glorious possibilities are wrapped up in these brown skins!

Lucius made a stirring talk one night. "A long time ago when the Gospel first began across the Big-water the devil was very mad. He tried to kill it like a prairie fire but he could not work fast enough, for it burst out in different places. It spread across the Big-water and came to the Kiowas. It kept coming, coming, coming, making a big bright light.

The devil was scared and ran on ahead like a coyote. He turned and looked back and then ran one way and another, giving out bad roads. He gave the whiskey road, the dance road, the card road, and the mescal road. To-day he is studying in his big bad heart what to do next.

It is the devil that tells the Ghost-Dance people just when Jesus is coming back. Jesus don't know Himself. When the right time comes the Great Father will call Jesus and say to Him : ' My son, it is time for you to go now,' and He will come back to this earth to finish up the business. We should all try to get our hearts ready for this."

Banked for building fund, $93.84.

March 10th. There are eight new puppies down in the dugout, all as black as coals.

March 18th, Sunday. We have taught the Indians that at all meetings the Holy Spirit is the Leader-Chief. He never comes late and when only two or three get in He is ready to help them if they listen in their hearts. He will call on different ones to speak or sing or pray and if they do what He asks them they will get a blessing. The missionaries are God's agents. They only read His orders, make them plain and then sit with the rest in the Holy Spirit's class to learn the spiritual truths.

We had given the ten commandments over and over again till many could count them off on their fingers. "What more does Jesus want us to do?" was then asked. They expected another long list and were glad to know that they were to learn one thing thoroughly at a time, next.

We gave a talk on "Confess your faults one to another." Paudlekeah arose and with thoughtful face said: "It is a wise road. Weak Christians fall. They should not hide it. They should come to the Jesus tent and tell their brothers and sisters. Then we will pray and get up and try all over again. I have spoken."

Long Horn didn't rise. He was sick and spoke lying on his back. "Some of you Christians don't talk straight. You come in here and give good talks to make the missionaries' hearts glad and then give your brothers and sisters bad talk. You better cut it off. If you are weak don't hide it. It is not straight to stand up in here and give sugar-talk."

Queototi: "I am a very quiet old man and don't talk much but I want to encourage the young men all I can, and confess. I have made two mistakes since I came to be a Christian and I want to tell it. One time we were out of matches and I went down to a white man's to

ask for some.   The door was open and nobody
was around.   I looked in and saw some matches
and took three.   I stealed them.   That was one
thing.   When I was going to the 'sociation my
wagon broke and I had no nails to fix it with so
I went to the blacksmith's shop to get it mended.
He was not there but I saw the nails and prayed
and told Jesus I was going to take them because
I was going to His 'sociation.   These are the
two mistakes I have made since I gave my heart
to Jesus."

Ananthy : " When I heard the Gospel first I
did not think it was for me, because I knew I
was mean and cranky.   I did not think Jesus
was looking for that kind of people."

Popebah : " The Great Father made the man
first and the woman last and that is why the
women are away behind."

Dawtobi : " If anybody points a pistol at your
head you must shut your eyes and pray for him
like I did for Poor Buffalo.   I just look into my
own heart and try to be careful."

Tone-gah-gah : " I can remember away back.
Our grandfathers were very wicked, fighting
white people and other tribes.   When I was a
young man I never heard one word about the
Gospel.   After I was discharged as a soldier I
came to Lucius to see if the report about a white
Jesus woman being here was true.   I was surprised that Miss Crawford was so leetle.   She

went down to the dugout and brought up some
patchwork and handed it to me.   I asked Lucius
how much it was and he explained that white
women who loved Jesus and wanted us to love
Him made it and sent it with their prayers.
That was the first time I ever heard about Jesus
and I came often to hear, because it was a kind
road.   After a while the Holy Spirit showed me
the way to believe and I gave my heart to Jesus.
Some of my people are mean and say : ' Why
don't you camp round with us like you used to ? '
I point to that mountain and say : ' The Great
Father has given me a home over there and I
stay at it and work.   I am one of the Lord's
children and His Holy Spirit will lead me as
long as I live.'   Then they laugh at me.   I am
really anxious about this other life in heaven.   I
will sing a new song for Jesus now.

> " God in Heaven
>   You are leading us,
>   In a safe way,
>   We want to be safe in your Home."

March 25th, Sunday.   A wagon filled with a
whole family drove furiously up to the gospel
tent and as soon as the singing and prayer were
over Doybi arose and said : " May I talk first
this morning ?   The devil has beaten me awful
bad and I told him I was going to come right
over to the gospel tent to tell on him.   Three

weeks ago he knocked me down.   You all know how hard I have tried since I became a Christian.   It was after payment and they were gambling in my tent.   All night they gambled and I laid down with the blanket over my head and asked Jesus to help me not to get up and gamble. That time I beat the devil.   I didn't gamble. Next day I said to my wife : ' Now we must go home to-day, for I want to get away from the temptations.'   She said : ' The Bible says we are to obey our parents and they say we are going to stay here and gamble some more, so if you want to go to Saddle Mountain you can go by yourself for I won't go with you.'   This made me awful mad and I took hold of my wife and shook her and knocked her down.   I stood there for a while and began to think of Jesus, and how sorry I was, for I love my poor wife very much. Then I remembered some of Jesus' words and I prayed and asked Him to forgive me and help me not to do such a bad thing again.   The devil is mean.   If he can't catch you on one road he will catch you on another.   I was watching the gamble-road and he caught me another way.   I have come to-day to tell all my brothers and sisters about it.   I am not discouraged.   Let us all keep close to Jesus and follow Him all the way through."

Papedone was on his feet at once.   " We have all heard about this before and we felt 'shamed for Doybi. When I heard it first my heart felt just like sick. Now if he had not been truly converted he wouldn't have come here this morning to tell on himself and the devil. It is because he is a Christian that he has come here and asked us to wipe it out. We are all one family and our brother has done wrong. He has asked Jesus to forgive him and he has asked us to pray for him. He can't do no more. I will kneel down now and thank Jesus because Doybi has got the real Jesus road in his heart. If he had not he would not have come here to talk."

Queototi arose. " I'm an old man," he said, " and have done a lot of work for the devil. He gave me bullets for it and I carry them in my body yet. I am thankful that Jesus has saved me. My dear wife has gone on to live with Him and I have brought her last Jesus money. I am afraid I have made a mistake on the Jesus road and I want to tell you about it. I try to stay home for Jesus' sake, but I have no one to cook for me now and I often get very hungry. A while back I was so hungry I did not know what to do so I went over to Hunting Horse's to get something to eat. He was not home and I was so hungry. I prayed and asked Jesus what to do and then I went back home and met the pigs running all over. I was very hungry so I prayed to Jesus again and said : ' Jesus, I am hungry and these pigs belong to my cousin. He is not at home or I would ask

him for one.   I am going to catch one and kill it
and eat it, but I don't want to steal, so I ask you
to look at me.'   Then I watched the pigs go by
and I catched the littlest one and killed it and
ate it.   Now I am afraid those not Christians
will point at me and say : ' Queototi is a Christian and he stole a pig,' and then all my brothers
and sisters will feel 'shamed.   I tell you about it
so you won't let the news spread.   I was hungry
and took the pig but I did not steal it.   I asked
Jesus to look at me.   What do you think ?   Was
it wrong for me to kill that pig and eat it ? "

Before I could reply Heenkey sprang up : "If
this spreads the others will say he stole the pig.
The deacons should pay for it."   Queototi's gray
head sank on his breast, his eyes suffused with
tears and his whole frame shook.   I went over
to him and said : "You dear old man, no, it was
not wrong for you to take that pig.   You did not
steal it.   Jesus knows all about it.   Hunting
Horse would have given it to you gladly if he
had been at home.   We all love you and know
you are trying to follow Jesus with all your heart.
You must not feel badly any more.   I will pay
for the pig just to make you feel happy again."

Gahbein : " We all must feel that Queototi
did right.   Don't let us speak it out.   We all
must feel that he tried to be honest in the Jesus
road."

Poor old man !   How his drooping head lifted

itself up after these kind talks and at dinner every one brought him the best they had. " Confessing your faults one to another " is the very best way to strengthen "the tie that binds."

May 26th. It is said that of all fowls the hen is the most religious because so many of them enter the ministry. Sometimes, however, they miss their calling.

This is my birthday and Miss Bare planned a " surprise " but had to let the cat out of the bag before time, because we were house cleaning. Having lived on scraps about a week we kept our courage up by thinking of the Big Eat ahead. Two chickens were killed, dressed and roasted in the oven in the shed. Every bit of the work was done and all was in readiness for the guests.

" Cheer up little Bear-woman ! I know you are nearly starved but we are in for a good square meal now. Good-bye to bacon, dried apples and beans ! Chick ! Chick ! Chick !— Chuck ! Chuck ! Chuck !

House cleaning is over. Company is coming. Hurrah for a Big Eat ! "

Miss Reeside and Miss Ballew arrived, Lucius and family were invited in and the meal served. There was no chicken ! Into the shed a dog had entered followed by eight coal black pups. Perceiving that the oven door was slightly ajar she scented the game. Not only was the pan licked perfectly clean but the corners gave no evidence of foul play.   Miss Reeside returned thanks.

Once in a while one who is expected to enter the ministry goes to the dogs but it is the exception.

June 6th. The bill to open the Reservation has passed the Senate.   Now for the tug of war !

It was midnight in the tepee ; the camp-fire smouldered and waiting relatives crouched with their feet in the ashes.   Suddenly there was a wild shriek from the bed and the whole encampment was filled with screaming.   In the dim light a man, stripped to the waist, could be distinguished seated on the rude bed.   A woman sat beside him clasping something in her arms. Tenderly he took it from her.   " My Way-behind-little-one ! My Way-behind-little-one ! My Way-behind-little-one !" he wailed.   " She is gone. My heart has burst !"   Lifting both tiny arms he placed them about his neck and clasping the body to his naked bosom rocked back and forth kissing, and kissing, and kissing the lifeless face. At intervals he stopped and raising his head towards the heavens poured forth lamentations of woe.

Through the rain the body was borne to the den.   At sunrise the parents appeared at the door forlorn and trembling.

Kneeling beside the missionary-box-coffin I

left them and hastened to prepare breakfast. There was no one at home. All had gone to town.

In the pelting rain the grave was dug and the funeral conducted in signs. Returning with the distracted parents, shivering and shaking from cold and exhaustion, I made them as comfortable as I could in Miss Bare's room and then went over to the den. I scraped the mud out first with a hoe then flooded it out with water and a broom and finally went over the floor on hands and knees with a cloth, twice. It was hard but not as hard as the sight of the stricken ones staggering down the bank of the creek towards their lonely tepee wailing, "My Way-behind-little-one! My Way-behind-little-one! My Way-behind-little one!"

June 21st–24th. The camp-meeting or Association is over. It was a big undertaking out on the bald prairie. The Indians worked hard, ate hard and prayed hard while building the great arbor and the missionaries worked like Turks clear through. We used quilt tops and linings basted together and filled with dried grass for bedticks, converted biscuit boxes into wash-stands, tea towels into towels, flour sacks into pillow-cases, bottles into candlesticks and the gospel tent into kitchen and men's dormitory. Three tepees were elegantly fitted up for Dr. and

Mrs. Murrow, Dr. and Mrs. Chivers, Miss Burdette and party. How they enjoyed them!

Mrs. Captain Parker and Mrs. Dr. Bonnell were the first to arrive from Chicago, followed quickly by missionaries, visitors and Indians from many tribes. Dr. Wm. Justin Harsha, a writer of Indian stories, from New York City, was also an honored guest.

A mountain climb was planned and on the highest peak a rock pile was reared. Surrounded by the kneeling company Dr. Chivers stood beside it and with bared head prayed— prayed that physical strength might be given— prayed that the church might be built—prayed for the Indians.

The meetings were an inspiration from first to last. After one of Dr. Chivers' soul-stirring talks Mrs. Hicks threw her arms about me saying: "Oh! We can never thank you enough for getting him here. His talks are just what we needed. Oh! I never have been so happy in all my life!"

Poor missionaries! Giving out, giving out, giving out the whole time. No wonder we feel spiritually starved at times! Nineteen happy converts were baptized in the natural baptistry in the mountainside on Sunday afternoon.

The farewells were said in the evening and in the morning the whole encampment melted away as if touched by a fairy wand.

Wrapped in his shabbiest blanket Domot visited the camp but once. "Tell the chiefs," he signed, with head erect and sorrow stamped on every feature of his face, "that my Way-behind-little-one has gone to sit down with Jesus. My heart is too sore to come to this happy place."

Camp-meeting receipts from Indian and white friends	$280.10
Expenditures	201.35
Balance on hand	$78.75
Quilts sold on the ground	19.00
Pelts sold	15.50
Gifts from visitors (unsolicited)	14.52
Grand total	$127.77

When the Indians heard this financial statement they were fairly astonished and voted to divide the money as follows:

To Baby Band	$15.58
To Lucius' salary	15.90
To sending the Gospel to others	15.88
To building fund	80.11

Then giving burst out afresh; $1.10 was brought forward for Baby Band, $2.85 for Sending the Gospel and $8.00 swelled the Building fund. I do not think there was a cent left in a pocket. They had given their all and were happy, although almost in a panic over the opening of their Reservation.

August 19th. Vacation.
Building fund, $238.60.

Lucius and Mabel Aitsan
(Lucius was ordained June 24th, 1913 and is now pastor of the Church)

Rev. J. S. Murson, D. D.

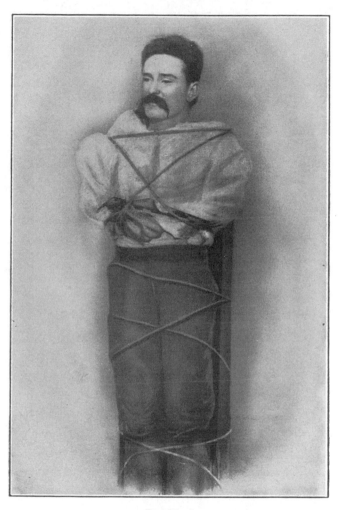

Red Buck

Miss K. E. Bare

Robert Burdette Spotted Horse

Rev. Robert J. Burdette, D. D.

Col. J. F. Randlett—U. S. Indian Agent

The Church

The Mission House

Kokom the Sexton and wife Pope-bah

Deacon Spotted Horse   Deacon Gal-bein and Son
(In native dress)

Deacon Tone-moh   Deacon A come-to
(The deacons all wear citizens' clothing now)

VI

Miss Burdette's Visit—Robert Burdette Spotted Horse—Incidents—Talks—Thanksgiving— More Talks—Dead-broke at Christmas-Time —A Gift from the Cheyennes and Arapahoes —Land Chosen—Government Appreciations

Saddle Mountain, September 14, 1900.

MISS CRAWFORD:

Dear Sister:—It is a very hard time for us now. Everything is turned upside down and I don't know what to do for my people. There is a lot of kick going on and some day you will hear something bad about us. This is not funny talk. It is not quiet here like it used to be. We are all troubled about our land. The Christian brothers and sisters are very weak and they told me to tell you this: "You say you work hard and are tired. You tell us not to ask you for what you got and to go to work and build our own church." They tell me to tell you this: "If you work till you are too tired to work you ought not to be a missionary. Stay where you are and take it easy." They say they will never, never, never ask you for what you got.

They are not feeling good and do not care for anything now. I'm sorry but I cannot help it. I only pray to Jesus to help me to be strong.

Your brother,

LUCIUS AITSAN.

September 16th. How glad they were to welcome us both back. We told them about the
people who wanted to shove Jesus over a hill
and kill Him because their hearts were blind
and they did not know that He was the best
friend they had. No application was necessary.
Indians don't like applications. They say they
have sense enough to think that part out for
themselves.

After dinner Lucius was the first to make a
talk : " We were so happy after the camp-meeting but when the missionaries both left us the
devil came along with a gun and shooted at us
and some of us got nearly killed. When a man
shoots into a bunch of quails some are killed
and some fly off and hide in the long grass.
When the man is gone the live ones call to each
other and soon they get together in a bunch
again. We are the same. To-day you have
come back and called us together again and we
are coming out of the long grass. I have been
feeling so bad but His words have made me
strong again and the 'heavy' has got off my
heart. Yesterday after I raked up under this
arbor I sat down and prayed to Jesus and said :
' When I gave my heart to you, Jesus, I put myself on your hand and told you to use me any
way you wanted and you made me your interpreter. We must not be discouraged but get
closer and keep trying, trying, trying and you

will give us our Jesus House and lead us on to everlasting life.'

My brothers and sisters, if we stay near to Jesus the devil will leave us alone. If we think we are strong enough to go around by ourselves the devil will steal us. Let us keep close to Jesus."

"I can see your faces from where I stand," said Heenkey, "but I cannot see your hearts or read your 'thinks.' Only Jesus can do that. It is a hard time for us now but I have been praying every day asking Jesus not to let us hurt anybody. You all know my wife. (She was present.) She is mean. She has an awful-big-mad but I ask Jesus to help me not to talk back and I remember my prayer. The Great Father knows our hearts. We must not stop to fight but push right on thinking of Jesus' own words. I have nothing to give you to make your hearts glad but I pray for you every night. This is my work for Jesus' sake. I have spoken."

September 17th. How glorious it was to welcome Miss Burdette to Saddle Mountain, even though she arrived tired and sick. As usual we had eaten scraps for some time preparatory to a company Big Eat. We prepared two chickens and had a nice civilized meal all ready when a white man from the camps all togged up in a clean shirt appeared smiling at the door and said : "I knowed you was going to have good-chuck to-night so I thought I would come up and eat supper with you." And he did.

On account of Miss Burdette's condition we just had one meeting and took her to one camp to name a three-day-old baby boy. The minute she took the young cherub in her arms and began to pray he began to howl. It was fun to watch the two faces. (I can't hear and have to look out to see when the "amen" comes.) The longer she prayed the more he yelled and the more terrific faces he made, for he was nearly frightened into fits. When the prayer was ended and the young sinner soothed the name was announced : " Robert Burdette Spotted Horse."

Then an Indian signed : "They ran a race and the papoose came out ahead. He's the chief."

October 8th. Indians all off. It isn't many days we get all to ourselves and when we do get one we make good use of it. We got up early and after breakfast Miss Bare pitched into the industrial preparations while I went at a variety of things. First I mixed down the bread, then patched a window pane, covered a box, cleaned the dugout, sorted supplies, made a cover for a barrel and chopped up a good big pile of kindling out of broken boxes. In emptying and refilling two candy buckets (in which we keep the flour), a mouse's nest was discovered, and everything in the room was turned inside out and bottom side up before the floor was mopped. When dinner was over the bread was put in the oven and nine and a half dozen eggs were greased to keep them fresh.

In lifting them to a shelf the box slipped and seven dozen of them floated their white and yellow insides all over the clean floor. Miss Bare didn't stand around with her eyes open and her hands up saying: "My! The very idea! I never heard of such a thing in all my life!" and then sneak off and leave me with the problem. She rolled up her sleeves and together we chased the golden sunbeams across the floor and up the wall.

There are people who go to the Bible in every time of trouble. I don't. After supper I took the cook book and hunted till I found a receipt for cookies without eggs and then went to bed comforted.

October 16th. Beathoma took me by the hand and leading me through two dirty rooms into a clean one, lifted a piece of purple velvet off a Bible and signed: "When a horse is tired and weak we turn him loose and soon he is all right again. I am the same way. This is my house and I try to keep it clean for Jesus' sake and teach my children to keep it clean also. Some days I am weak and tired and give up but in a few days I clean out every place again. I cannot read the Book but I keep this room clean always and oftentimes I come in and look at it and ask the Great Father to let the Holy Spirit teach my heart the same that is written in it and make His road plain to me."

October 20th. Lucius made a talk to-day that was unique. "This is Jesus' tent and we come in here to worship. Some of you talk and laugh and say funny things and it makes Jesus' heart hot. When you come in you should put all your 'funny' behind you and not look back, and try to think Jesus all the time. We should take our 'funny' off at the door, face the Jesus Book and listen good to what Jesus tells us. Then when we go out we can pick our 'funny' up again and go off with it, but 'tain't right to bring it into this Jesus tent."

Said another, "Every time I see this tent I think how poor we are with only a tent for Jesus and it is getting old. I am glad to hear Jesus' words in it though for that is what makes me strong. When I do wrong I will come and tell it."

"Cheer up, cheer up! Jesus doesn't notice the old tent. It is your new hearts He is interested in. When He sees you doing without a Jesus House to send the Gospel to others His heart laughs.   Cheer up! cheer up!   Everybody laugh with Jesus."

Heenkey: "One question I want to ask.   Does the Jesus Book say that Christians should carry revolvers?   Many of the Christians are buying them and carrying them round.   White people are coming.   I want to know what the Jesus Book says."

"It is not right for Christians to carry revolvers."

November 18th, Sunday.   Splendid attendance, attention and testimonies.   Here are some of the talks:

(1)   "The Great Father has forgiven my sins and given me a house to sit down in.   When we come over the lonesome road and see other houses with nobody in them we feel sorry because all the Great Father's 'kind' is losted.   Once I got up to talk for Jesus at another place and the Jesus man sang to make me stop talking.   It was the devil that told him to sing so I talked on for Jesus and beat them both."

(2)   "The Ghost-Dance Indians think that Jesus is coming back here to live and will give them back their dead and their buffalo.   It is not true.   Jesus will never sit down here again. When He comes next time He will come to judge everything.   He will put the sheep Christians on one side and the goat Christians on the

other and then burn up this whole business and take the Christians and little children up to heaven."

(3) " The old roads are passing away. How glad I am that I was not born a long time ago. I remember the war-path and the buffalo. The Indians went all round fighting and taking scalps. Once they brought a black man's scalp home and put it up in a tree. I was so skeered I could hardly sleep and dreamed about it. Now how different it is. How thankful I am that Jesus sent the missionaries to tell us the Gospel. The old roads are passing away and how happy the Jesus road is."

(4) " No matter how far the devil chases me I will come back to Jesus. He drove me to gamble this payment but I held tight four dollars for Jesus. I don't know why I am so wicked. Sometimes I get awful mad at my husband and scold him and kick him and abuse him but after my heart gets quiet I always forgive him."

(5) " When you told us Jesus wanted us to forgive our enemies I thought of Paudlekeah right off. My heart is turned against him and I cannot turn it back myself. I tried but when I went up to him I felt so mad I couldn't speak so I shook hands. After a while I think that I will be able to go and pray with him and then the bad will all go out of my heart, but 'tain't gone yet."

(6) "I am surprised to hear all these good words about being kind to everybody and not to lie or steal or give bad talk. I been thinking all that before I heard the Jesus road. I believe also the Great Father wants us to work and earn our living."

(7) "When Sunday comes we all know it now. We are learning something new right along. I have found out this: If anybody is against us we should shut up our mouths because we are Christians. A while back I made a mistake and want to tell my brothers and sisters about it. A calf died and my wife and I went to see if we could cut some meat off it. When we got back home the key was lost and my wife and I began to abuse each other. She packed up and said she was going to leave me. I stood looking at her, burning in my heart and I said to her, ' The devil is leading you all right.' The tears ran down my cheeks but she started and I was left alone. When she got as far as Sugar Creek the Holy Spirit came into her heart and told her to go back to her husband so she turned back. We did not feel good for several days, but one day when we were eating a watermelon we got all right. It was the devil that got in between us and tried to pull us apart, but Jesus is stronger than the devil. This is how I have been serving Jesus."

(8) The wife: " I have a bad temper and the

devil chases me all the time. Before we built our house we kept happy going round. The way I got mad was this: He is the man and he lost the key and I told him he done it. Then he said something and I said something back and we kept on talking at each other. Then I said, 'Now I'm mad and I ain't going to get over it. I'm going to leave you.' I started but when I remembered my talks over here I knew it was the devil and I pulled my horses away from him and came back. I know I done wrong and I felt I should come to tell it. I said to the devil: 'You knocked me down all right and beat me but you ain't going to keep me down. I'm going to get up and tell on you.' This is what we done last week for Jesus.

Once I got up to talk for Jesus at another place and the Jesus man sang to make me stop talking. It was the devil that told him to sing and I talked on for Jesus and beat them both."

November 29th. Our first Thanksgiving. (We are careful to make it understood that Sunday is ahead of all other days.) I made my talk first, thanking Jesus especially for my two noble yoke-fellows, Miss Bare and Lucius. "Every time I look at either of them my heart gets big with thanksgiving."

All had something to be thankful for but this is the talk that interested me most. "I have

four cousins and none of them are saved. I
thank Jesus for giving me this special work to
do for Him."

The thank offering was $11.65 and Robert
Burdette Spotted Horse held the audience spell-
bound with his music when his money barrel was
handed back and wouldn't rattle. The mother
looked so embarrassed I signed : " It is all right.
He must catch the giving-to-Jesus-road when he
is little or he will make a bigger fuss than that if
he catches it when he is big." She was twice
thankful.

November 30th.   Early this morning we started
for Cache Creek fifteen miles away and before
dinner one quilt was set up in the yard. While
the women were washing the dishes the men
worked on it and then taking their guns rode off.
Three quilts were finished before the hunters returned with two large wild ducks and numbers
of quail. After sundown, by the light of the lantern, set on the bottom side of a lard pail, we
gathered in the tent for a Big Eat.

We girls fairly gorged ourselves for we seldom
have the chance to fill up on things we like.
There weren't knives, forks or spoons enough
but we borrowed from our neighbors, loaned and
used fingers and thumbs, enjoying the civilizing
effect of being Primitive Methodists for once.
How our faces shone with the pure oil of glad-

ness! (and of duck).   No one could have distinguished us from real Indians.   Every pick was demolished except the bones, which lay in higgeldy piggeldy piles with dishes, pots and pans as if the result of a volcanic eruption.   Under these conditions Miss Bare gave a splendid talk and the host responded :

"Once you gave my wife bread medicine (yeast).   She mixed it up at night and cooked it in the morning.   It made our teeth tired.   It is all true what you tell us about Jesus.   I am lost unless the Holy Spirit leads me to the light."

December 3d, Sunday.   Some of to-day's testimonies :

(1) "All Jesus' days I get up early and wash myself all over.   I comb my hair and clean myself from my head to my feet.   When I am through I ask Jesus to look at me.   Then I sit down and *think Jesus till it is time to get the horses for service."*

(2) "The devil is like my own brother and stays with me all the time.   When I am ready to talk about Jesus I take him out of my heart and lay him down.   After I have prayed he comes back in again."

(3) "I am a poor losted sheep but I like to come here to listen.   It is hard for me because I have two wives but I can't help it and try the best I can."

(4) "Sometimes on the Fourth of July some horses look so nice that everybody says: 'Yes, that horse will come out ahead,' but some old ugly horse beats him. Christians are the same. Some of you dress up so fine, maybe you think you look good, but in your hearts you are away behind and some ugly Christian with poor clothes will come out ahead."

(5) "You all know me. I am so weak. You are God's sheep and I am like a poor losted one. I have strayed away from Jesus and I don't want you to scold me. If you help me I may come back. A worm on a tree feels round for something to take hold of and then he jumps over. I am the same way."

(6) "All the time since I started to follow Jesus I have tried to get close to Him but somehow I got stuck and went back. The Great Father punished me and sent a cyclone to destroy my house. I cannot talk to others now because they will say: 'Look at yourself. The devil knocked you over all right.' I cannot talk but I can pray for them." (One hundred dollars was raised for him to rebuild.)

(7) Jimmy Foxtail came forward with one cent. Holding it aloft he said: " I put more money than this away for Jesus but the devil made me spend it. I want you, my brothers and sisters, to know that if I had not held on to this tight the devil would have had it too. He's awful mean."

(8) "My little boy has gone to live with Jesus. This twenty-five cents is his last Jesus money to Baby Band."

December 16th. In sending our October salaries Miss Burdette wrote : " Be careful of your money for I don't know when you will get any more. The churches and circles are slow in sending their offerings and the bank has shut down on us." As Christmas drew near we watched the irregular mails anxiously. Finally we could wait no longer and drove the twenty miles to town. On the way in we ate our dinners from a lard pail (as we hadn't a cent among us) and then drove direct to the post-office.

The biscuit box mission-mail-box was full. Sorting the letters we tore them open one by one, just glancing at the contents. Some told of boxes and barrels sent for Christmas, others told of personal interest in the missionaries, etc., but the majority were requests for special letters for Christmas and New Year's celebrations. When we were through *we looked at each other*, gathered up our belongings, got into the hack and were taken to our hotel. It was quarantined with smallpox ! " Yes, we have room for two more," said the proprietor of another hotel ; " fifty cents for the bed and fifty cents for the meals and you can't have the bed if you don't take the meals." That settled it. Lucius drove to the camps and we sneaked out and sat on a box at the door till the last mail for the night was distributed.

It got dark but we had been recently vaccinated and carried firearms so were not afraid. The corner saloon suddenly burst into light. Seizing the Bear-woman I said "Hurrah! Free lunch! Here's our chance. Come on."

There was no money in the mail. We went to a friend's. Her face literally burst into smiles when she opened the door and saw us. She and her husband had repeatedly asked us to make their home our stopping place when we came to town and this was the first time we had accepted the kind invitation. " Come in! Come in! Come in!" she said. " Welcome a hundred times!" and then she hustled around and prepared the most delicious city supper. It took a little time of course but never once did either of us say, " Don't go to any extra trouble for us. We can eat anything." For we were cold, hungry and penniless. We couldn't talk, but how we laughed after we were tucked in the comfortable folding bed in the parlor. The springs heaved as if the pigs were running under them. First one would laugh, then the other, then both.

In the morning we went to the bank and borrowed ten dollars. When the man handed it out I asked: "What do we do next?" "Nothing. Just pay it back when you can." " Don't we sign any papers or mortgage our clothes or

anything?"   "That is all right," and the banker
laughed a good big laugh.

The freight bills were twelve dollars, and Christmas candy six.

December 25th, Christmas. Kneeling beside
the tree and emptying his pockets on the money
table Lucius prayed: "When I gave my heart
to you, Jesus, I gave you myself altogether and
I asked you to use me any way you liked. To-
day I can say thank you, to you, Jesus, because
you have used me right and brought all these
people into your road. As long as I live this
life, Jesus, use me right. Don't use me for anything wrong. And, Jesus, you know I never
say to you: 'Give me this good thing or give
me another good thing.' I just follow you as
my Leader and trust you to take care of me.
Whenever I get some little money I always lay
some beside me for you, Jesus. I never forget you.
And now, Jesus, I want you to do one thing for
me. When I get into any temptation and I call
your name 'Jesus! Jesus! help me!' you must
help me right off. You know my heart and all
about me. If my heart faces away from you I
want you to pull it round. You have been kind
to me, Jesus, bringing the missionaries right to
my house, so I will do all I can for you as long
as I live."

He gave five dollars to send the Gospel to

others saying, " If we build the church first it will be too late for the old people."

Robert Burdette Spotted Horse dropped in his coin without a groan and when the giving ceased the treasurer broke open the barrels. In the hush that followed a woman's voice was heard in prayer.

"Jesus, save the unsaved givers. Jesus, help us with our church; the tent is getting old. Jesus, I am not a strong Christian, I am weak, so weak." The money was then counted.

Baby Band, $11.40. Sending the Gospel, $17.45. Lucius' salary, $17.90. Church, $54.10. Total, $100.85.

The days following Christmas were like the days preceding it—full of labors oft, with medicine, meals and meetings all mixed together in hurricane style.

January 19, 1901. Gahbein found me in the dugout and leading me to the light signed: " The Great Father has been kind to me and given me a boy." Then in broken English and signs he said, " In the Book an old man had a son. I savy the big name Abe-ham. I call my boy Abe-ham."

February 14th. We left on the third and are just back from payment. It rained and snowed, gamblers were thick and a smallpox scare broke up the camp.

"When you are through eating," said two white men pushing themselves into Lucius' tent, "we have brought whiskey and want to gamble with you to-night."

"You must go some place else," was the reply, "for none of us in this tent do those bad things."

All worked hard on the quilts. We tied off and sold eighteen, dividing the money evenly between sending the Gospel to others and the building fund. Including the Christmas and Thanksgiving monies we sent $75 to the Jesus Women Society and banked $93.77 for the Church. ($12.50 of this last amount was a free-will offering from Chinese of San Francisco and Oakland.)

February 16th. Gahbein is back with the smallpox and my sister and her husband from Toronto have come on a visit. We have quarantined the gospel tent.

February 24th. To-day we had the regular services in the tent and listened to very interesting talks.

(1) "Last Sunday I saddled my horse to come to service when I heard we were cut off and I felt pretty bad. Then I heard there was to be no services again to-day but I couldn't stay away any longer, for I have not heard any

of Jesus' words for four weeks. When Washington orders the soldiers to fight they expect to be killed but have to obey. The Great Father is our Washington. He orders Christians to go everywhere with the Gospel and be 'skeered' of nothing. It is not right to be skeered of small*fox*. Jesus does not tell us to ever shut up His tent or His Book."

(2) "If I was Miss Crawford and could read I would not be afraid of small*fox*. She should go and read and pray with Gahbein."

(3) "A long time ago when a chief was afraid of anything we put a rope around his neck, cut off his ears, and never let him be chief again. It is all true what the others have said. Jesus sent you here to help us and now you are skeered of the small*fox*."

When they had all talked themselves out we replied : "Jesus expects us to use the sense He has given us. Suppose we went to see Gahbein and got the smallpox and gave it to you and all your children, what then? Bring the rope. You can have the ears. Jesus never asks His children to be foolish."

They all saw the funny reference to the *ears* and good nature was restored.

March. Hip! Hip! Hip! Hurrah! We certainly have had a big surprise to-day. Our good friend Dr. Roe of the Dutch Reformed Church

Colony, Oklahoma, read our Christmas letter to his Cheyenne and Arapahoe Indians and they wanted to help with the building fund. A day was set for an offering and so eager were they that one man and his wife stood by to see the money counted. When they heard it lacked a little of being twenty dollars the woman gave forty cents more and the man pledged the balance. Another man gave one dollar and still another, unable to be present, sent seventy-five cents. With the Sunday-school offering the total amounted to thirty dollars.

Hip! Hip! Hip! Hurrah again!

Dr. Murrow also sent ten dollars for the church. Greatly to the Indians' consternation we spent every cent of it in quilt material instead of putting it in the bank.

With the money Dr. Murrow wrote: "I would gladly have our Indians send you something but I am so heartily in sympathy with your ideas about teaching them to work for what they need that I prefer hands off. I have seen so much sit-down-and-do-nothing among the Indians and wait-for-somebody-else-to-do-for-them that I glory in your spunk to inspire them with the necessity of per-spring. The truest and best friends of the Indians are those who will persistently, and perhaps contrary to their will, train them to the habit of work and self-reliance. Keep your course firmly, lovingly, laughingly.

Be not the least bit disturbed. The Indians cannot understand your course. Do not expect it."

April 2d. To-day Lucius was out all day selecting the allotments for his family. Every man, woman and child is to get one hundred and sixty acres of land. Riding up on a hill he got off the horse, knelt down and prayed : " I can do nothing without you, Jesus. Choose the land for me and don't let me make any mistakes. All that I have is yours, Jesus, and you know I never forget you. I want my cows to have calves and when I get money I will give you some. Choose the land for me and then I will go ahead."

May 12th. The council is over and the land for the church given. The business was not ours so we only made a little talk, urging the unsaved to give their hearts to Jesus, as He would sooner have them than the land.

Domot, representing the unsaved in the vicinity, spoke first. " I am a poor sinner with two wives but I want my children and grandchildren to walk in the Jesus road. Jesus is getting the good place ready for us and we must give Him good land. I am not good to plough but I am good to think in my head and in my heart. We are crowded for land over here but we will give Jesus one hundred and sixty acres of land, eighty

near the graveyard and eighty somewhere near.
I have spoken."

Lucius spoke for the Christians, and made the
official prayer, which in the Indians' eyes completed the transaction.   All shook hands—the
great council was over.

May 12th.   The land for the mission was selected.   Eighty acres in one fairy spot and
eighty in another, half a mile apart.

The law prescribed that " all missions already
occupying land " should be granted titles to a
specified number of acres.   We were occupying
no land at Saddle Mountain.   It was through the
untiring and determined efforts of our masterful
agent, Col. J. F. Randlett, at one end and Commissioner Jones at the other that our allotment
was secured.

The kindness of the government officials has
been marked all the way along.   Every courtesy
that could be lawfully granted has been extended
not only willingly but gladly.   Besides the land
for the mission, the agent and Inspector Nesler
put their heads and hearts together and located
one of the four Kiowa cemeteries next to our
mission property (including the lone tree).

In his annual report to Washington Colonel
Randlett had this to say under the head of " Missions " : " All have done well, but the mission
conducted by Miss Isabel Crawford under the

patronage of the Women's Baptist Home Mission Society of Chicago deserves special mention.

Miss Crawford has spent nine years at her isolated station (including three years at Elk Creek), surrounded by no other inhabitants than these Indians and with the single young lady associate in her work for companionship. The theme she instructs upon is that the Master worked and that those who would follow Him must work also, and that able-bodied Indians should be producers of the necessaries of life, thereby attaining self-support and ability to help those who cannot help themselves.

Early in the commencement of her mission work she announced that her worship of God while with them would be in open air or tents until the time should come when from their own contributions and labors a house could be built for that purpose. Her following now has about $400 deposited in the bank for that purpose, her Indians following well her example and precepts. Her efforts are appreciated and praised by all who have known her and it is gratifying to everybody to know that she has recently been recognized by the Department and established with a conditional missionary title to land for her mission."

I copy most of this report not so much to exhibit the feathers in our own caps as to demonstrate the fact that much to the contrary there are Indian agents who are thorough gentlemen and appreciative of the work of others.

Commissioner Jones wrote : " I want to congratulate you heartily on the outcome of the assignment of land at Saddle Mountain, but it was a close call. . . . If it had not been for the fact that I had visited you and knew personally the conditions surrounding the mission the matter would have failed. But knowing as I did the good work that you have been doing among the Indians the secretary finally consented to approve the allotment."

May 31st. Vacation.
Building fund, $362.37.

VII

*Camping—Opening of Reservation—The Moving
—A Midnight Funeral—A Letter of Sym-
pathy—The Hopi Mission—The Rock Island
Gift*

JULY 1, 1901. To your tents, O Israel!
One, two, three and away we go to Rainy
Mountain school for the grass-money.
Such a procession! No circus could compare
with it. Wagons, hacks and buggies were filled
with men, women and children, bedecked in
brilliancy, rivaling sun, moon and stars. Boys
on horseback, shirted in pink, purple, red, green
and yellow with gay feathers in their hats and
girdles elaborate, dashed in and out and round
about herding the loose horses attached to the
procession, to remove temptation from the incom-
ing whites.

An old woman astride a spotted pony rode
here, there and everywhere trying to protect us
with her "medicine-bag" from all the evil spirits
in existence and out of it.

Down we went, "not close by" or "near to"
Saddle Mountain Creek, but right into it, pell-
mell and out again with the same lightning speed.

What's the matter now? All the rigs turned
aside and waited.

Lucius, their leader, remaining behind to clean
up the yard, drove to his place at the head of
the procession. The rest fell in line and the
boys scattered over the prairie to round up the
herd. The wild horses snorted as they were
driven in, slashed their tails and almost stood on
their heads. The others caught the spirit and
away we went bumping from side to side, laughing and signing as if fairly intoxicated with life
itself.

> " How the wild crowd went swaying along,
>   Hailing each other with humor and song."
> How the gay schoolboys like meteors flashed by
> Bright for a moment then lost to the eye!

Suddenly the trail was left, every wagon taking a different direction and the prairie was
dotted over with men, women and children gathering wood.

Ropes were thrown over dead branches and
pulled crashing to the ground, axes were swung
high in the air bringing down limbs that only
leaned earthward, and in an incredibly short time
every wagon had a wood-pile extension on behind
and was speeding back to the mountain trail.

Two hours for dinner by a spring under an
Indian arbor and away we went followed by
barking dogs and crazy horses. When almost

in sight of the school the procession scattered again, this time to hoe down tall grass for the beds. Huge bundles were hoisted on top of the wood-piles and then down came the rain. Next day "God's-Light-Upon-the-Mountain" burst forth in splendor. All day long the women worked at the quilts tying off nine and selling them for thirty-seven dollars, a day's record unsurpassed in the annals of the tribe.

Every night gospel meetings were held and every day rain or shine quilts were tied off and sold. In all thirty-one comfortables were finished and eighty-six dollars taken in from the sales. The climax was reached when the report was given of Dr. Murrow's ten dollar gift to the church. It had been invested in batting and linings. Thirteen crazy quilt tops had been pieced out of odds and ends from the missionary barrels and when tied off, twelve of them sold for five dollars apiece and one for two dollars and fifty cents. Total amount, $62.50.

Fifty-two dollars and fifty cents was banked for the church and ten dollars reinvested.

An Indian arose: "I have a dollar to give to the church," he said. "Don't put it in the bank, for it will sit still there. Spend it and *let us work* and it will grow bigger and bigger."

Lucius gave eight dollars, another man one dollar and Wee Colonel Randlett gave one hundred cents before he was twenty-four hours old.

The total cash receipts from the trip were $169.50 ($81.30 for the church).

A camp-meeting followed the payment at Rainy Mountain Mission eight miles from the school. Spotted Horse (a future deacon), father of Robert Burdette, was baptized and Lucius made the following remarkable talk : " I want to make two talks. In the first place to the new Christians and the second place to the old ones. I understand Jesus has a book and He has written your names down in it who were baptized to-day. When a white man wants to send a message to Washington he sends a telegram. You must send a message to Jesus often to help you. Every day send Him a message very often and to-night before you go to sleep thank Him for writing your names in His everlasting book. It is a long way up high but He will hear you.

Now I will say a few words to the old Christians. Some of you are very near asleep but I want you to rub open your eyes and listen. The devil puts you to sleep so you can't hear God's words. You been hearing a lot about Ghost-Dance and mescal but I will tell you some more. We all ought to be honest Christians but we are not. Some of you hide your money and do not pay your store bills. You been stealing from the traders when you don't pay up and I am 'shamed of you. Some of you keep away from your store bills and buy things

for your body, so when others see you they will
say: 'How-look-pretty-you-are!' This is not
right. The devil makes you do it but Jesus
wants you to pay up.

When you get your grass money you should
first lay by some for Jesus, then go and pay up
your store bills and spend what is over on yourselves. When you don't pay up the traders are
mad and I feel awful 'shamed when I hear them
talk about you. Another thing, I want you to
remember that you have a new road altogether.
You have houses and homes and you must live
in them and keep them clean. You should
clean up the yard every day and the house
and keep at it, keep at it, keep at it and never
get tired.

Another thing, when my shirt has a little
hole in it I ask my wife to put a patch on it. It
is not right to buy new things all the time. We
all have some old clothes and we don't throw
them away. We keep washing, washing, washing twice a week. Jesus gives us water free and
soap and you men ought to help your wives to
wash and keep the children clean. I wash for
Mabel often and it isn't hard work. We don't
buy new things all the time. We keep washing,
washing, washing and mending till the things get
too old and then we don't throw them away;
we make dish rags and try all the time.

Some of you wear your shirts till they get

dirty and then you throw them away and get new ones, and that is why your store bills are so large. I want you to have one good suit of clothes for all your children for Sunday and for yourselves and when you come home put them away. I've had this suit three years but I take care of it.

Another thing, I want you men and women to be kind to each other. Some of you get mad and talk back. When your husband is mad and talks cross to you make your hearts strong and don't say anything, and pretty soon he will be sorry and say to you: 'My dear wife, I did wrong when I gave you bad-talk; will you forgive me?' and how happy you will be; but if you talk back you will both get mad and it will get worse and worse.

My brothers and my sisters, let us try hard to be clean on the Jesus road. Let us keep our hearts clean, and then our clothes and our children, for the Jesus road is a clean road and we have to keep at it all the time or the devil will make us dirty again.

The old road has passed away and we have a new road altogether."

On the way back to Saddle Mountain we noted a sign-board set up on a fresh crossroad bearing a black hand pointing to the one word "Cooper." It was the first evidence of the beginning of a new life. Miss Bare saw it first.

The border towns were filled with land seekers years before the Reservation opened and tent villages sprang up suddenly as the time drew near. The claims estimated to be thrown open for settlement were not half enough to go round but all applicants were allowed to register and received numbers.

At the end of a specified time these numbers were placed in a box, a little boy turned a crank and as they dropped out the corresponding names were published. August 6, 1901, the Reservation opened and the "lucky-numbers" poured over the prairie like burning oil set afloat on an open sea. On horseback, on muleback, on shank's mares, in wagons, in buggies, in gigs on they swept, lashing and slashing and urging their beasts, with faces burning and perspiration and hair flowing.

There was no ordinary "Onward Christian Soldier" attitude about them. They meant business. Fires were started in every direction to find the corner stones, flames shot into the sky and swept whirling across the plains, smoke darkened the sun. Only the trails were safe and they were cut into such deep ruts and pitch holes that life was not safe driving faster than a walk over them.

As seventeen carloads of liquor had been shipped to the new towns, whiskey bottles, broken and empty, were in evidence everywhere and with dust, ashes, cinders, smoke, fire and the mad rush it was not hard for the Indians to imagine that the day of doom had surely come.

Before reaching Saddle Mountain most of the excited multitude had scattered north, south, east and west, up, down and all over. The sites for three county seats had been selected before the opening and these were the objective points for most. Lawton, thirty miles away, was the one nearest to us. Such a place! No one could imagine it. The lonely prairie over which the missionaries had travelled so many times, became a city in a night. There were four hundred places of business and fifteen hundred tents before a lot could be sold, a daily paper the first day and over ten thousand inhabitants before the city was two months old.

The Presbyterians were the first to organize a church. Our wagon had scarcely stopped when a man pushed up with a basket of doughnuts for sale. A basket of doughnuts! Think of it— for sale on our desolate prairie! Peanut stands, lemonade stands, jewelry stands and saloons (one swinging a sign: "Welcome to all nations but Carry") were everywhere.

A group of men surrounded an old white nag that was being auctioned. Some one bought him for $4.50, and as he was led off the mob hooted till the sky nearly split.

There were cripples and deformities, beggars

and bootblacks and a circus wagon advertising "A flying woman" (as if that was anything new). "Lawton Laundry," "Oil and gas," "Pabst Beer" blazed forth on up-to-date business wagons. Streets were named and stores were numbered, yet there was not a building in sight. Tents, tents, tents, nothing but tents as far as the eye could see.

The two land offices of course were the centres of attraction. At El Reno a man made $480 in three weeks with five tubs in a tent, charging twenty-five cents a bath.

Great crowds surrounded the office at Fort Sill. Only a limited number were allowed to enter at a time and the police were kept busy holding the rest in check.

Fruit sellers passed in and out through the crowds but men seemed too busy to eat. Apart from the multitude little groups formed round men who stooped down and marked off claims on the ground with sticks.

Tobacco in all forms was a common commodity. Hardly a man or boy was to be seen without a pipe, a cigar, a cigarette or a quid. Razors and soap did not seem to have struck the country yet.

Sixty days were allowed for the "lucky-numbers" to choose their claims. After that the "unlucky-numbers" were allowed to come in and seize upon any odd acre overlooked or ignored, and then the general public was admitted. Hundreds gathered at Owl Creek October 5th to await the appointed hour of midnight. There were clean men and dirty men, shaven men and unshaven men, exhausted men and fresh men, men in white shirts, men in black shirts, collared men and uncollared men, cuffed men and uncuffed men, men with gold watches and diamond rings and men with revolvers and spurs.

There were big women and little women, navy blue calico women and red calico women, women in white and women in black, women in sunbonnets and women in hats, and children from tiny infants up. In and out among the people stood saddled horses and vehicles of every description.

A woman made a camp-fire and cooked bacon in a long-handled frying-pan filling the air with appetizing aroma and presenting a picture fit for an artist's brush.

A man who had evidently called at " Welcome to all nations but Carry " took a long drink out of a bottle, rolled himself up in a quilt and lay down under a tree.

Late comers brought last reports from the land offices, causing fluctuations in interest in certain circles. The marvelous part of it all was that there was no disorder, no roughness, no rowdyism, no unpleasantness of any kind. That great excited multitude handled itself without the aid of a single policeman. About ten o'clock the "sooners" began to move off quietly to be near the land they had "spotted." The moon was due at 11 : 29 but rain threatened and the night was pitch dark. Men in ambush, striking matches to see the time, made the creeks look as if they were alive with fire bugs. At the exact hour of twelve the grand rush for claims began. Stakes were driven, names and dates were deposited, hats were waved in the air and away the crazy crowd dashed for Fort Sill, running, jumping, climbing on horses two or three at a time and springing unbidden into fast passing conveyances or hanging on behind.

Hours before the land office opened there was a long line of waiting, anxious, tired-out, frisky people. First comers took first places. All were supposed to have registered.

"How much will you take to change places with me?" a man asked the one ahead of him. "Five dollars?" "Not much! Nothing less than fifty dollars." Exchanging places on down the line Mr. Sharper went, simply raking in the cash, and when he got to the end had enough to buy a farm. And he belonged to the last class of "unlucky-numbers" without the right to file.

We reached home at half-past two in the morning. Opening my satchel I was confronted with an empty whiskey bottle, labeled: "Rich and mellow. America's finest production."

America's finest production is the Indian, not alas rich and mellow, but poor and despised! It is time now to ask how he is taking this onward march of civilization with its fresh evidence of Christianity. Proud, haughty and determined he stands, trusting for the most part in this fine agent, his missionaries, the Great Spirit and his shotgun. Ready at a moment's notice to fight for " the land where his fathers died," and fight to a finish—the finish of himself.

Domot expressed it exactly when with trembling hand he signed: " We are afraid of everything that is coming except the Jesus House."

The next exercise on the programme was the moving of the den to the church property. It was hoisted on two long skids attached to eight wagon wheels and moved the mile free of charge by professional house movers assisted by Indians. The chimney fell off and the doors and windows were wrenched but nothing more serious happened. I followed on the last load of our belongings.

Miss Bare was off visiting churches but the mover's family occupied the tenant's house at the foot of the hill so that I was not alone. The first night I slept on " a heap " surrounded by other heaps. In the morning I lifted up mine eyes to the hills. Oh, glorious vision! Myriads of mountain peaks pointed upward to Him and the blue of the sky and gold of the sunrise vied with each other in casting a fairy mantle over all. It was strengthening to stand in the midst of chaos and confusion, knowing how long it would take poor human efforts to bring about order, and think of Him who spoke and it was done!

They were short a man for bringing over the shed and the mover's wife and I offered our services, which were accepted. It took the whole morning prying the thing up and getting the wheels under it. Finally the four horses were hitched on and followed by a flock of Indian children, barking dogs and grunting pigs we drove full-sail out of the yard. All went well till we got to the creek. It was thought that the speed gained going down one bank would carry half-way up the other, and I was stationed on a log spanning the water to block the wheels when they began to back. Down the others came with their mighty load. The skids struck the opposite bank full force! There was grand scatteration! The four horses almost turned somersaults backwards. The shed balanced in the air a moment and then came down whack on the woman's skirts. The man jumped into the creek and I fell into mud and slime over my elbows up to my nose. No one was hurt, so after laughing till we couldn't laugh any more and chopping and tearing the woman free we went to work again and succeeded in getting out of the bog.

The second crossing was easy and after it was passed I scampered on home to see about the bread which had been worked down before we started in the morning. As I opened the door the moonlight fell on fold-on-fold of the fluffy dough draping itself all over the table. None of it had quite reached the floor, so making a charge at it I wisped it all up, worked it down and put it in the pans. Then I lit the lamp. What I saw was nobody's business.

We were all so stiff and full of bumps, lumps and splinters in the morning that we were glad to eat any kind of bread even if the "Gulf·Stream" could be traced in every slice.

The days following were full of "labors oft" that Paul didn't know anything about because he was a man. I was glad Miss Bare was out of the mess and yet I needed her.

First I emptied the den into the shed. Then I swept the ceiling and walls, cleaned the windows, washed the woodwork and book shelves, scrubbed and oiled the floor and ate beans.

La Junta, Colo., had taken my measure and instead of packing a missionary barrel packed a missionary box that looked like a coffin for Goliath. It took half a day to make the cover for it and adjust the hinges and another half day to pad the top and cover all with pretty cretonne. A hook in the under side of the cover and an eye in the window frame completed the job. A little tick was made for the bottom, a feather bed, soft blankets, white sheets, pale pink comfortable, pillows with lace trimming and Eureka! I was the owner of my first real bed in Oklahoma!

The books were next unpacked. Poor books! I confess there was rebellion in my heart as one by one they were tenderly lifted to their respective places. Once I thought I couldn't live without reading and at graduation promised myself that I would spend fifty dollars for books every year of my life. I did it once. Freight bills on missionary boxes and barrels and absolutely no time for self-culture prevented the repetition.

The bath-room (13 x 5 feet) was a sort of combination pantry, grocery store, clothing establishment and apothecary shop. In close proximity might be found lard and liniment, pickles and paregoric, sugar and salts, corn-meal and corn plasters, bottles and beans, dishes and disinfectants, dried apples and dry-goods, pills and potatoes.

The cutest little china cupboard was made out of a biscuit box, a piece of white oilcloth and a dark green silk throw. The extension table underwent repairs and cleaning and when it was placed across the front window with a pretty cover on it, and Miss Bare's white enamel bed with white counterpane arranged, I felt as if I had been transplanted from a jungle to the palace some people sing about in connection with a tent.

During the operation of getting settled I had worn one and the same dress and towards the end there was more trimming on it than the style required.

The first morning after the shedding the tenant's dog failed to recognize me and ran growling and barking down the hill as if he had been scalded. I bore him no ill will, for he only emphasized the fact I had heard over and over before, that returned missionaries even in their best looked like frights (*to other frights*).

Miss Reeside and Miss Ballew came to spend a Sunday. How glad we all were to welcome these heroines of the chase, and how proud I was of our new quarters—till supper time came. While the rain danced on the shed roof and the wind blew through the sixty-four big cracks like a hurricane I tried to cook.

The mover's wife hoed a furrow round the stove to let the puddles run off and then held a lantern while I stood on a board, fork in hand. The contents in the frying-pan sizzled and sputtered wickedly as water dropped in from above and steam rose from some place below as if a boiler had burst. At last the meal was prepared and as I passed out of the shed with both hands full the great door gave me a parting bang on the back and held on to my skirts till the wind nearly carried the food down over the hills. How fortunate it is that company never knows what goes on behind the screens and how glad I was when I got to bed with both head and feet aching, that I didn't have to make those two ends meet.

Next in order was the twisting of the den straight. Although the land was all surveyed there were no roads or fences to guide us so it was an interesting operation. Every man in the country knew exactly how it should be done and volumes might be filled with instructions received.

An old-timer called and told me of a new settler over near him who wanted to make a dugout. A man from Nebraska told him how to dig it, a man from Kansas told him how to wall it, a man from Indiana told him how to roof it and a man from Texas told him how to fix the door. He followed every direction *exactly* and, as the cattle man said, "had a Jim Dandy of a place with everything off."

At twelve o'clock the shadows of the sun are supposed to fall exactly straight. All morning we pried and pushed on the building and about noon waited. Every watch was different! Arguments followed and when the men were too tired to argue longer, all agreed that the sun was "about right" and with one gigantic effort the house was swung into position.

The tenant sank a missionary barrel in the spring for a well and I sank a biscuit box beside it for a larder. How proud I felt as I placed a heavy stone on the plate on top of a big earthenware crock full of lard, butter, eggs, etc., in the ice cold water. In the evening, going out to bring in the washing—hung on the bushes near the spring—I found that a Mrs. Pig had been there before me apparently suffering from a very bad cold in her head and feet! A few days later I heard tramp, tramp, tramp on the veranda and opening the door was confronted by a whole regiment of little black pigs. All that saved the mother as she splattered the cat's milk right and left was the fact that she was a poor grass widow with a large family and no visible means of support.

It was Saturday once more and cold. Breakfast was just over when word was brought in that a white child had died in a tent seven miles down the creek. Driving down we found a woman surrounded by a lot of crying children, ragged bedding, pots and pans and on a board resting on two logs the body of a little girl about six years of age. The father was away hunting for land, but was expected back any minute and the mother did not want the child buried till his return. Assuring her that it would be all right and that the Indians would be glad to let the little one rest in their cemetery, I offered what sympathy and help I could and then went back to the usual Saturday scrub work and cooking.

About sundown the door burst open and in

swarmed the whole bereaved family, clothed in tatters and screaming at the tops of their voices. The child had died of smallpox and they had been ordered to bury it at once. The body was in the wagon outside. Disinfectant was freely used, missionary barrels were ransacked for warm clothing and the Sunday dinner was placed on the table. Without the aid of knife, fork or spoon the meal was ravenously devoured and then all drove up to the church in the dark in the wagon with the box.

Two white men dug the grave. The children and mother cried and cried and cried the whole time. The cold was intense.

Finally the men climbed out of the grave, took off their hats and leaned on their shovels. Trying to master my feelings I opened my mouth to speak but my teeth chattered so that I had to stop. Then I cried and when I got home at twelve thirty cried again. There was no stove and no fire. Next morning was Sunday. Montahahty was dying and the services were held about her death-bed under Kokom's arbor. I came home weak all over and after eating some cold scraps dropped into the sleeping box on my back too tired to turn over. Suddenly there was a great rattling noise outside. I started up but was not afraid for I remembered that Miss Bare's bed springs had been placed against the house on the veranda. The wind was rattling them, that was all. Louder and louder, harder and harder the banging became, every thud striking a nerve. Finally I dragged myself up and going out held on to a veranda post with one hand while I laid the springs down flat with the other. The wind was terrific but by holding on to the post till I got a grip on the window frame I finally succeeded in reaching the door. It banged shut in my face with the latch-key on the inside! I couldn't go down the hill to the tenant's house barefooted in the dark, and I couldn't lie down on the springs. What was I to do? After stubbing all my toes and skinning both shins I finally succeeded in reaching the shed with its sixty-four ventilators, opened the big doors that had no hook on the inside, found a cot and a quilt and laid down to wait till morning. First I lay with my face to the wind, but the half of the quilt that wasn't under me suddenly unfurled like a flag in a stiff sea breeze. Then I lay with my back to the wind and a corner of the quilt nearly picked out an eye. Finally I arose, wheeled a missionary barrel to the side of the cot, stacked the contents on top of the quilt to hold it down, and slid down into place. Every garment was lifted in the air and sent whizzing against the wall. The next move was successful. I made a barrel organ of myself and *put on* everything; men's clothing, women's clothing, boys' clothing, aprons, hoods, handkerchiefs, throws, flour sacks, pen-wipers, iron holders, rags, batting, patchwork and socks. What would not go on I *filled in.* Then I laid down and held possession. At daylight a man was to call for the mail, but before he came I had smashed a window pane and reached my clothing.

November 11th. The chimney was repaired and the stove was moved in.

November 23d. Miss Bare returned and we decided to "grin and bear it" to the end (she of course to do the latter). Thus endeth the chapter on how the missionaries at Saddle Mountain were greatly moved.

DEAR COLONEL RANDLETT:
We are in great trouble in our neighborhood because the Great Father has taken from us our dear sister Kokom's daughter, Montahahty. She has been sick a long time with consumption and Friday night at six o'clock Jesus came for her and left all our hearts crying.

To-day we have heard that a great sorrow has come into your life because your boy whom you loved so dearly has had to suffer again. We are only poor Indians and cannot help you any but we feel that we can tell you we are sorry for you and for him.

When a big storm comes up our horses often bunch together between the mountains and stand with their heads down trying to keep each other warm. A great storm of trouble has come upon you and upon us lately. Let us put our hearts together and with our heads bowed down try to comfort each other under the shadow of our mighty rock, Jesus.

We are poor Indians and cannot help you any but we can promise you that we will try to be good citizens and not give you any trouble. If one or two of our Saddle Mountain Indians do wrong do not think we are all in it, for we are not, and we are ashamed of them. We try to do right for Jesus' sake and when we make a mistake we are all sorry.

We put our hearts beside yours in your trouble and we pray that both you and your boy may meet us some day in the home Jesus is preparing for us all.

Written on behalf of Daw-kee-boom-gee-k'oop Missionary Society, Saddle Mountain, Oklahoma.

Lucius Aitsan,
Secretary.

November 24th, Sunday. After speaking from the words, "Go ye into all the world and preach the Gospel to every creature," we told of Miss Burdette's wonderful trip to Arizona in search of the other tribe to which they wished the Gospel sent before building their church. With eyes bulging out of their heads they listened, and the moment the talk was finished prayers of thanksgiving, songs of praise and testimonies burst forth.

(1) "God's-Light-Upon-the-Mountain has borned a papoose! Miss Burdette had named it

Sunlight-Mission.   God's-light and Sun-light
Good ! "

(2)   " We have had great news to-day.   Now
the old people will hear the Gospel and be saved.
If we had built our church first they would have
died and been lost and it would have been our
fault."

(3)   " It was the Holy Spirit who told us to
send the Gospel to the other tribe *first* and we
are glad we listened.   Jesus' sheep at Saddle
Mountain have been scattered lately but this
good news will bring us together again.   A
white settlement has come in among us but we
must not mind it for Jesus will stand with us."

(4)   " I believe this working for Jesus is the
biggest work in all the world.   We must pray
for our missionaries every day and ask the Holy
Spirit to teach them what our poor hearts need
most."

(5)   " The Hopis are like our own children because we sent them a missionary.   We hear that
their hearts are like stones and they are deaf in
their two ears, but we must not get discouraged.
We must keep on praying for them because we
are trying to spread the Gospel.   They worship
snakes.   The snake is the devil's friend.   He
tempted Eve and Adam and the Great Father
punished him and made him crawl on the ground.
Kiowas hate snakes and kill them every time
they get a chance.   The Hopis are poor but if

they find Jesus He will help them. The first thing they must do is to open their hearts and let the Holy Spirit in, and then go to work for Jesus."

(6) "I am thankful to Jesus for taking care of Miss Burdette. She had a hard time but He brought her through all right. It is in Odlepaugh's home that we heard the news. We must all pray earnestly for his grandchild, Robert Burdette."

(7) "My heart is so happy to hear the great news. I've been working with my hands and have brought forty-five cents to Jesus for His church."

(8) "We are hungry for a Jesus house. The gospel tent is all wore out. We sent the Gospel to the others first, now we must pull hard on our church."

"No! no! Wait! Wait a minute!" I interrupted. "There are other tribes still and many people across the Big-water who have never heard. We must never put ourselves first. We must push just as hard as ever to send the Gospel to others."

Heenkey arose. Poor Heenkey! "When I come over here on horseback since the gospel tent tore down I don't know where to go. What are we to do?

Dr. Murrow knows about us and so do others. Why don't they talk it over and help us? I want you to take down my words and send them to Dr. Murrow."

An answer came back immediately. "Miss Crawford sent me your letter and I am glad to get it. I am always glad to get a letter from any of the Kiowas. You want a church-house; that is right. You and your people deserve a church-house. God will give you one but you must be patient. God's time has not come yet. Your missionaries are wise women. They love the Kiowas. They will work hard for Saddle Mountain. Be patient. Good things grow slowly. When God's time comes He will direct His servants to arise and build a house for His service. My heart is with your heart but let us wait on God."

One week later we met again in an Indian house. They listened as Indians always do listen, to a talk about the bad spirit that pulls us down and the good spirit that helps us up.

The work of the bad spirit was illustrated this way: A man was walking down the road, followed everywhere he turned by a lot of pigs. He carried a bag of beans and dropping them as he went the pigs followed blindly after him.

The devil throws out here and there along the journey of life enjoyments which coax his followers on to destruction.

The work of the good spirit was illustrated thus: Away across the Big-water mothers, anxious that their children shall not waste time, give them knitting to do and wind in throughout the balls shining coins and little pretty things so that when the fingers might grow weary and throw down the work,

" From out the ball will drop the hidden gift,
To please and urge them on to search for more."

"Jesus knows we are like little children, needing encouragement along the way while trying so hard to build a church for Him and to-day He has sent us a great present." Breathlessly they listened to the reading of the following letter:

MY DEAR MISS CRAWFORD : I am just writing to tell you a pretty little story about a ride I took yesterday with the president and directors of the Rock Island Railway Company.

The vice-president, Mr. Parker, wired me that the train would pass here at 12 : 30 and invited me to join them on a trip to Lawton. I closed my desk and went with them—was just away three hours. On the way up from Lawton Mr. Parker kindly inquired for you and the prospects of your mission. I told him you were prospering in your labors but under trials and tribulations that were enormous, but that you were not disheartened. Those of the gentlemen who listened to Mr. Parker's praises of you and your young lady associate became much interested when he remarked that you ought to be helped with funds to enable you to commence the construction of your little church building.

This resulted in one of the party taking out a twenty dollar bill and saying : " Here is a starter ; let us raise the two hundred dollars she needs."

One of the young gentlemen went out into the other car and in a few minutes returned with the cash in his hands and handed it to me to deliver it to you. When he counted it into my hand it was found to amount to $240. A Mr. Cabel then pulled out a ten dollar bill and made it $250. By this time I began to feel my pig nature aroused and said to myself : " I wish I could have told them she needed $400 instead of $200, for I know those kind-hearted fellows would have handed it out cheerfully."

As I was leaving the car Mr. Parker said : " Now tell Miss Crawford that we raised the two hundred dollars to go towards the completion of the church building but the fifty dollars in excess she must keep and devote to comforts for herself and her assistant."

Now my happy story ends. What say to the Doxology ?

With congratulations, I remain,

JAMES F. RANDLETT,
U. S. Indian Agent.

Heenkey was on his feet at once with consternation written all over his face. " You all remember," he said, " that I asked Miss Crawford to write to Dr. Murrow and tell him how hungry we were for our Jesus House. He sent words back telling us not to be in a hurry, to wait on God and He would give us our church in His own time. We prayed to Jesus till we were all wore out telling Him to talk to the *Big-water people* (Baptists). He has talked to new hearts altogether. The people with the little-water-road spread on their heads have helped us. We send thanks to these kind friends and from now on we will ask help from Jesus only."

The treasurer got right up as soon as Heenkey sat down. "I take charge of the Jesus money," she said, "and every time I get any I ask Jesus to look at it. I am happy to-day."

All Lucius could say was, "We feel jumped (surprised) and say thank you to Jesus first thing."

It was the turning point in the history of the church building fund. There was no more begging or groaning.

Ah-mot-ah-ah had a question: "Why did the Great Father give out so many Jesus roads, Catholic, Methodist, Presbyterian, Baptist? Why did He scatter us like that? Why didn't He make one strong Jesus road?" The matter was explained according to history and great excitement followed the statement of facts. When quiet was restored Ah-mot-ah-ah again arose: "In the middle of the summer let us call a big council and get in all the Methodists, Presbyterians, Episcopalians, Catholics, and their missionaries and you talk to them from the Book and look into their two eyes and don't give up till you beat them. Then we will make one big strong Jesus road and all the Kiowa Christians will walk on it, for we want to please Jesus only. While you talk we will pray and Jesus will help us." I replied : " It is not a wise road."

With a crestfallen look that nearly upset my equilibrium Ah-mot-ah-ah again got on his feet. Looking at me as if I had been suddenly proved guilty of murder in the first degree he turned to the people and said and signed : " She's skeered ! " and sat down. Some one else signed : " It is true ; she was skeered of smallfox." Dinner followed.

Christmas, 1901. An Indian in an old faded garment came up to the front and said, " You all know my sister Montahahty is dead and the Indian road would not lead me to this happy place to-day. I came for just one thing : to tell the unsaved about Jesus. If I do not do this when Jesus comes He will say to me : ' You are my servant ; why didn't you tell those people about the true road ? ' Then what will I say ? "

One hand was raised for prayer.

The birthday present was as follows :

To sending the Gospel to others,	-	$ 43.08
To Baby Band, - - -	-	15.02
To Lucius' salary, - -	-	16.90
To church building fund,	-	104.20
Total, - - - -	-	$179.20

April 6th. Vacation.
Building fund, $747.87.

VIII

Giving the Gospel to the Whites—Wood or Stone?
—The Hauling—Election Day—The Laying
of the Corner-Stone—The First Wedding—
Christmas 1902—An Important Camping
Trip.

AUGUST 24, 1902. The day began with
a carnal conflict and ended with a spiritual victory. At sunrise a wagon drove
up to the house of the Interpreter and the driver
said :

" Good-morning, Lucius. I understand you
have big meetings over here every Sunday and
last night I killed a beef. It is nice and fresh
and I thought you would like to buy some for
your dinners."

" You must excuse us," said Lucius. " We are
Christian Indians and don't do any trading on
Jesus day. You will have to sell to the white
people."

At eleven o'clock we had our regular service.
A bunch of cattle worried by numberless church-
going dogs came in on the gallop and surrounded
the arbor while the Indians were singing. As if
by common consent every animal wheeled on
the dogs, shook her horns and stood listening

with head erect. The music ceased, the cattle walked slowly away, the dogs crept under the seats and the service continued. At the close an invitation was given to all who felt strong enough to come to the arbor at night and give the Gospel to the new settlers to do so. It almost created a panic.

" White people are dangerous," they said, " they laugh at us and will come with sticks and revolvers and act crazy. The road is too hard."

The night was dark, lanterns were hung in the arbor and about forty white people gathered in neat clothing and with faces full of kindly interest.

The lesson was from Acts ix. 1–23.

At the close of the prayer Lucius arose. His face was set and his breathing short. After a few nervous twitches about the mouth and arms he said : " You all know we are Indians. We lived in the darkness for many years but our Great Father was kind to us and sent us the light. To-night when you were coming you were in the darkness till you saw the lanterns over here and then you turned and followed until you got under this arbor. We were the same way. We saw just a little light at first but we hunted and hunted and now I am glad to say we are in the light. We are weak yet. The devil beats us many times but we try all we can to follow Jesus. I am not ashamed to stand before your faces to tell you that I am saved, because I know it. I know I am a Christian for God's Holy Spirit has come into my heart and He makes me know that I am saved. You white people know everything. You can read the Bible for yourselves but some of you are in the darkness yet.

The Great Father sent the only son He ever had to die for you. Why don't you love Him and give Him your hearts? Jesus came to this world to seek poor sinners. He did not come for only Indians or only black men or white people. He did not come to look for skins. He came to look for your hearts and mine and everybody's. We will pray for you that the Holy Spirit may show you the way."

Kokom spoke next. "I am a Christian Indian but I don't know much. When the country opened for settlement a lot of white people came in here. Some of you are Christians and some are very bad people. We don't know yet which are the good and which are the bad but we hope to know soon and then the Christian Indians and Christian white people must stand together and try very hard to find the poor sinners and bring them to Jesus to be saved.

If you make fun of me I'm not ashamed, for the Holy Spirit tells me to stand before your faces and make this talk. If you laugh I can't help it, but I will pray for you and ask Jesus to forgive you and give you new hearts."

Not a person laughed or behaved himself unseemly from the beginning of the service to the close, only the wolves kept up a blood-curdling howling from the hills that seemed uncomfortably near. Next day one of the neighbors came in and said, "When Lucius was talking last night Joe B.'s eyes were busted in his head."

I said: "What was the matter with you, why didn't you help us sing?" "I didn't want to spoil the music," he replied. "You can't hear but as soon as you began the wolves began. When you stopped to jaw us, they stopped and when you sang, they howled too."

Later in the day Joe B. called and said: "I always thought before that the Indians were very ignorant, but last night I got my eyes open. Lucius' talk surprised me very much. That fellow knows what he is talking about and so do the others. The white people in here don't understand the Indians, they know more than they think they do."

September 2d. Banked $40.80 for the building fund.

September 29th, Sunday. The lesson was on the building of the temple. For the first time in my life I could see nothing wonderful about Solomon's prayer. Under such circumstances, what else in all the world could he have prayed for but wisdom? We are asking for the very same thing but it certainly is not because we are so good or so unselfish but simply because we need the wisdom and know where to get it.

"We have studied over all the business," we told the Indians, "and we have found out that if the Kiowas will get the rock out of the hills we can build a beautiful stone Jesus House."

Buffalo Pants sprang to his feet. "You—you —you two white Jesus women," he hissed, "have made the stone-road all on the sly and now you want the Kiowas to vote for it. The hide-road is yours and you can walk on it yourselves, for we will not walk on it with you." Nevertheless the majority voted for stone. The minority were not expected to help in any way and they were expected to stand off and criticize. It is an Indian road.

Asking for additional wisdom we brought the matter up again. "If the Indians will all pull together for a frame building the missionaries will pull with them."

"What? what? what? You no catch 'um stone, you push 'um lumber? You no get mad and pull away? It is a new road."

"Jesus wants no bosses in His church," we replied. "Some of you voted for stone because you thought the missionaries would not push for lumber. You let us boss you and you were wrong. The business is yours and we have only two votes. Remember that the strongest Christians are those who can give up their own way and walk on a road they do not like in order to keep the weak ones in the bunch." All voted for the frame building.

October 3d. It rained fearfully and the roads were terrible but Lucius is an expert driver and we reached Apache, twenty-five miles off, in safety. Finding the lumber office we handed in the specifications, asking that the estimates be sent by mail.

Just as we were about to leave town I remembered that we needed a new dust pan, so depositing a sack of apples and another of eggs on the back seat of the hack, I hopped out and made the purchases. Returning I beheld Lucius, Mabel, Leslie and Richard all eating the apples. Climbing in again I sat down good and solid on the eggs. The dogs barked, the horses slashed their tails and away we went over the muddy road scattering golden sunbeams all along our way.

October 5th, Sunday. The discussions were most interesting. All eyes were screwed into interrogation marks when it was announced that we must visit other towns and ask for estimates on lumber. "The other churches were all built for the Indians," we explained. "You are to build this one yourselves and look after every

bit of the business. When the different lumber-
men tell us what they will charge then you must
choose the one who will give you the lumber
cheapest and best."

All were in arms at once. " It is a crazy road
to go running all over as if we had no sense.
The chiefs we go to and do not buy from will
all be mad at us and at the chief who gets the
order and it will be our fault."

" It is not being a Christian to make these
men fight." These were only some of the splendid Christian unbusinesslike things that were said.

Gotebo, a little town twenty-five miles away,
got the order.

Two good contractors were secured. Tonemoh
was appointed " Hauling Chief " and Odlepaugh
" Wake-um-up-in-the-morning Chief."

Excitement surged like the waves of the sea.
Odlepaugh said he couldn't sleep because his
heart kept hitting him so hard and turning him
over and over and over again and he had to
start one day ahead of the rest.

October 17th. Bright and early at a given
signal wagon load after wagon load poured out
of Lucius' gate like shots out of a gun, followed
by big dogs, little dogs, black dogs and yellow
dogs all barking and bounding into the air as if
they too understood the importance of the mission. Away the procession went into the creek

and out of it, up-hill, down-hill, around the mountain and out of sight. Every man, woman and child of the Indian population went; all had given and all had the right to haul their own lumber.

A dozen of the Rainy Mountain Christians helped and Tah-noity let the camp be made on her allotment.

"My throat is busted," said one returned hauler as the rain poured off his hat. Cough medicine was given him.

"My back is busted," said another with water swishing out of his shoes. Liniment was handed him.

"I'm all busted," said number three, dripping from hair, ears, nose, chin, coat sleeves and coat tails. A bottle of patent medicine, warranted to cure every ailment under the shining sun, was presented and the happy soused company started off again signing:

"The devil is trying to beat us with rain, but we won't give up." And they did not till all the hauling was done for both church and mission house, seventy-nine loads in all.

Aycompto (a future deacon), Doymah, and Tonacho were baptized on the trip and a baby girl was born. We called her Church-Bell but the Indians signed: "She is the little-wise-papoose - who - got - here - in - time - to - help-with-the-hauling."

NAMES OF HAULERS

Lucius, Mabel, Leslie and Richard.
Odlepaugh, Ananthy and Grace.
Tonemoh and Guestomah.
Spotted Horse, Hattie and Robert Burdette.
Heenkey and Gahyad.
Dawtobi.
Doybi and Keza.
Frank Doybi and Johannah.
Herman Bah-lah.
Hunting Horse and Beathomah.
Tonacho and Katie.
Akometo, Doymah, Malcolm, Philip and Church Bell.
Samuel Ahtone.
Long Horn and Willie.
Queototi and Robert Onko.
Amos Aitsan and Kaun-todle.
Big Tree.

Sainco.
Toybo and wife.
Mr. Wind and wife.
Jimmy Foxtail and wife No. 2.
Moses and wife.
Kiowa George.
Gahbein.
Little Robe.
Ahtonah and son.
Ahmahaha.
Tonegah-gah and Keapetate.
Papedone and Sapmah.
Ah-horn.
Henry Long Horn.
Tahnoity.
Andrew Stumbling Bear.

November 4th. (*Election day.*) The Indians dressed in their best swarmed the poles at Sugar Creek. They were tepee poles, for the other "pole" and the three beeves that had been promised did not materialize.

After dinner I made my maiden political speech. "The Great Father has given you men votes to use as soon as you know how. Indians have lost their lands and brought trouble on themselves by hurrying up to touch the white men's pen. It is not right to sell your votes for beef or anything else. The white men who told you to come here to-day have the devil's brand on them and were afraid to come to this meeting.

It is right for you to vote for good men and good laws but not till you know who the good men are and what the good laws are. Keep your votes as a present from Jesus. Never sell them and use them only when you know they will make this great world better."

Sore over getting no beef and glad to hear that the white-men-liar-chiefs belonged to the devil, the crowd slowly scattered and we returned to Saddle Mountain satisfied with our day's work.

November 9, 1902. (*The laying of the corner-stone.*)

Singing, " The Mission of Jesus," Gotobo.

Prayer, Queototi :

" Jesus, we thank Thee that we have come together for the corner on this church. We don't understand what it means to put our names in this tin box but you are the Chief and you have brought us together on this road. I am an old man but I stand with these young men. I want you to send the Holy Spirit among us to guide us. To-day we are gathered around our new church to get it started. I have been very wicked and a great sinner but to-day I am saved. I have spoken."

Scripture reading. Psalm 100, Amos Aitsan.

After the opening services the Indians with faces keen with excitement climbed over the piles of lumber and pressed as near to the foundation as they could get. Lucius Aitsan, secretary of Daw-kee-boom-gee-k'oop (God's-light-on-the-mountain), read the history of the work at Saddle Mountain, outlined as follows :

April 12, 1896.   Work began.

June 19, 1897.   First arbor built for Jesus.

November 16, 1897.   The gospel tent set up.

May 10, 1898.   Daw-kee-boom-gee-k'oop organized.

July 19, 1898.   First money given to Jesus ($17.26 towards sending the Gospel to another tribe and $17.34 towards the church building fund).

October 4, 1898.   One hundred and sixty acres of land promised to Jesus.

June 21–24, 1900.   The Association met at Saddle Mountain.

May 12, 1901.   Land for Jesus selected.

August 6, 1901.   Reservation opened.

November 17, 1902.   Sunlight Mission born.

November 9, 1902.   Corner-stone of church building laid.

When the reading of the history was completed the manuscript was placed in a tin box and the Indians passed up dropping in their names and the names of all who had contributed towards the building whether living or dead, present or absent. Mrs. Tonemoh, President of the Missionary Society, put in a block of patchwork and some buckskin and beads. Mr. Heenkey, the Vice-President, another block of patchwork, a piece of china painting and small pictures of Paul sewing on a tent, of men chopping down trees for the temple, and of men, women and children giving money to Jesus. The Treasurer, Mrs. Dawtobi, dropped in the original gold dollar and ten cent piece. Mrs. Aitsan put in a Bible, Mr. Doybi a Kiowa hymn book, Mr. Queototi a "Sunlight Mission" pamphlet, Hester a Church manual, and Minnie a copy of *Tidings* containing the names of all the Head Officers of the Women's Baptist Home Mission Society. A flock of little Brownies then came up and put in the names of Commissioner Jones, Inspector Nesler, Colonel J. F. Randlett, Brigadier-General F. D. Baldwin, Dr. Robert Burdette, Rev. and Mrs. Clouse, Misses Reeside, Ballew, McLean, Williams, Jensen, Mrs. Stevens, Mr. and Mrs. Dunn, Grand Forks Baptists, Buffalo Baptists, Chinese of San Francisco and Oakland, Cheyenne and Arapahoe Indians, of Colony, Okla., the Rock Island Railroad, and last but not least Mr. Papedone lovingly placed the names of Dr. and Mrs. Murrow with the rest. On the top of all was laid a colored photograph of little Stella Stumbling Bear who passed to be with Jesus the day the foundation of the church was begun.

The box was closed and placed in the cavity prepared for it. The contractor filled in small stones and mortar till all was covered and then Miss Bare, placing the large stone on the top and tapping it with the trowel, said : " I pronounce this stone well and properly laid."

Kneeling with uncovered heads on the grass, on the gravel and on the lumber piles, the voice of the interpreter was heard in prayer : " We thank you, Jesus, to-day, because you have been kind to help us get started on this our church. It is the first day we meet here for worship. We want you to forgive the mistakes we have made, pass them back behind you and help us to get stronger, so all the Indians will see the light get brighter and brighter. Keep your eye on our names so the devil will not scratch any of them out. I have spoken."

Mr. and Mrs. Aycompto and Mr. Tonacho, the Indians who had been baptized when off for the lumber, were asked to come forward and there beside the unfinished building they were given the heart's-right-hand-of-welcome, some weeping, some praying as they took them by the hands and others making a more joyful noise unto the Lord.

Thus ended the service connected with the laying of the corner-stone of the long-dreamed-of church, but no pen can describe the effect upon the Indians. Their natural love of ceremony reached its spiritual climax and when all was over they scattered like the breeze filled and thrilled with religious enthusiasm.

Thanksgiving day dawned clear, cold and frosty. The wagon came for us early and the load was made up of bread, pies, dishes, fruit, contractors, missionaries, Indians, wedding cake and a preacher. The building was floorless, windowless and almost everything-else-less, but boards were laid across the joists from vestibule to the front, and a piece of carpet spread so that the bride and groom might walk in style and safety.

The bride was gorgeously attired in pink, green, orange, yellow, red, purple and blue and waited modestly and sweetly while I skirmished for the bridegroom among a crowd of giggling boys. They told him if he was going to be married the white-way he would have to take Kaun-to-dle by the arm and march her in. As Minnie (or Kaun-to-dle) wore a blanket, to take her arm meant to take all of her, so Amos, son of Lucius, hung back.

Three times I got him to the door only to have him break loose and run, while the minister and friends waited inside. Stepping up to Lucius I signed : " Sing and stand where I can see when your mouth shuts." He shifted his position and began to sing and I went out and collared the youth. Standing behind him, holding both of his arms tight, I said, " Amos Aitsan, you are going in this time if you go in head first."

He giggled, looked from side to side and stood helpless a minute. Before he had time to make another break Lucius' mouth shut with a snap and with my head on his back he was carried clear through the vestibule into the church. By the time he gained his equilibrium Kaun-todle was beside him and the ceremony proceeded with becoming solemnity.

There were just eighteen wagon loads of Christmas barrels and boxes hauled out by the Indians and freight bills amounting to $106 paid by the missionaries out of their own pockets. (Refunded through the courtesy of Captain A. H. Parker later.) The station agent said if there was any place on God's earth that there wasn't a missionary barrel from he'd like to know it.

The old gospel tent had been put up over the house lumber so that we had a little extra room in it in which to unpack and repack. (We put by enough things for next Christmas.)

Armful by armful we carried the contributions into the den to be near the fire and stacked the little place almost to the ceiling. (Indians are not the only people who " heap-sit-down." Several of the pairs of pants sent in were " away behind.")

There were many personal remembrances. Just why one missionary should be remembered more than another is a question. I counted it all up and figured this out : If the Bear-woman had had twelve noses in a row down her spine I could have hung upon each a calendar, a blotter, a sofa pillow, a pen-wiper, an apron and an iron holder, to say nothing of handkerchiefs.

Before we were through ticketing we were cold, hungry, cross and cranky. It is not the actual gospel work that uses the missionaries up, but combinations of unlooked-for experiences and aggravations. Our swill pail is kept in a space between the house and the shed, the tenant emptying it every evening. In the midst of the rush a pig escaped from his pen and upset it right across our path. We removed it to the shed, putting it on the top of an old stove and next day a dog found it and brought its whole contents down over the Christmas things. Something else upset the ash pail and something else tore open a sack of corn-meal. We had no time to clean up messes, eat, sleep, mend tears or rub on liniment. We got like hornets. The devil beat us all right but we kept right on with the work.

The " strained conditions " between us finally came to a climax one night after midnight. I had not been able to sleep and as usual spent the time counting over money I didn't have.

Ten cents of the building money could not be accounted for. Suddenly I remembered that it had been spent for extra shingle nails. Getting up cautiously I lit the lamp, arranged the shade so the light would not strike the Bear-woman's face, put on shoes, stockings, and a warm wrap and with the books and a pile of unanswered letters went to work. I wrote on a long, long time and then turned round for something. There sat the Bear-woman clothed, if not in her right mind, scribbling away like a steam engine! I was flaring mad and said, " That is a nasty mean trick. I'm going to get myself out of this room as fast as I know how, and sleep in the bath room, so you won't be disturbed again! Sneaky mean!"

Dragging the bedding out of the box by the roots I got half-way through the door when the Bear-woman quietly said: " You don't need to move. I'm going to the gospel tent for the rest of the night." With one bound I cleared the feather bed, got out the door first and was off for the tent as fast as my legs could carry me. A tick full of rolls of batting from the different barrels and boxes and a few blankets and quilts had been thrown on the top of the lumber pile, so it was not long before the change of atmosphere caused me to fall into a gentle doze. Suddenly the lumber shook. A bright light struck my face and fumes of sulphur entered my nostrils ! Goodness ! Where was I? Was the Bear-woman going to burn the lumber to smudge me out ? The match died and another was struck. Hanging on to the lumber with one hand and holding the lighted match to her mouth with the other, the Bear-woman enunciated very distinctly : " Do-you-want-me-to-go-home-to-morrow ? "

The match went out.

" No, I don't." Another match was struck and held in position.

" Then - you - get-right-up-and-come-back-into-the-house."

" I won't do it. I can't sleep in that old stuffy place. I'm all tired out and I was just going to sleep when you—bo-hoo, bo-hoo ——"

Half an hour later I paddled back to the house, made a good face at my sleeping partner, and putting the bedding back, crawled into my box and slept like a top till morning.

The church was unfinished. Ceilings and windows were absent but not forgotten. Burlap bags and old quilts were nailed over the openings and the heat from the one small stove was hardly perceptible. One of the talks almost upset us.

" The devil pulls people this way and that way but Jesus pulls us one way, straight ahead. The Christians are going ahead all right. Look at Lucius. He has a Christian home and how glad we are always to come and see him. See our white sisters. They are just *like men and angels.* They have good sense and are very smart."

Heenkey : " When I was a young man I never heard a word about Jesus or the Book. It was after the missionaries came that our ears were open and we began to locate our farms and build fences. This is how we heard about Sunday. We were cutting poles and Mokeen called out, 'Stop! stop! We must not work to-day.' When I went for my horses another man said, ' Don't work to-day ; just cry to the Lord.' He was against Christians and this was funny talk. This man stands very high to-day in the Jesus road. He used to be strong for the devil but now he is strong for Jesus. I will call out his name : Kokom. About the same time there was a mescal eat near Saddle Mountain and I was there. After I became a Christian I went again to talk to the young men about Jesus. One of them said to me : 'We don't want any of your talk and we don't want you to come here. We eat mescal and gamble and dance and we don't want your advice. Our hearts are our own and we can do what we please.' One day after that I saw that young man in here and he said : ' I used to walk on all the bad roads but I have given them all up.' I will call out his name : Dangerous Bear. I used to be the same as these men I have been talking about. I want the missionaries to know that I tried to stay away from Jesus but I couldn't do it. He brought me in. Jesus is stronger than the devil. There are just two things I like ahead of everything else—coming to church and working on my farm. These are the only two roads I walk on now. I love it! I love it! I love it! I cannot stay away. I tell you I love this church and I try to walk straight for Jesus' sake. I have spoken."

At the foot of the tree crouching on the cold bare floor beside the missionaries and interpreter an Indian woman and three young men professed heartfelt conversion through the power of the Holy Spirit. Kneeling beside them Queototi gave to Jesus His usual birthday gift.

Sunlight Mission, $15.30; Baby Band, $13.80; Interpreter's salary, $13.55; Church, $66.35. (Total building fund, $855.02.)

But the joy in the presence of the angels of God was over the four sinners repenting more than over the $108.99.

February 2, 1903. It was impossible for both of us to leave so the Bear-woman made the road to stay at home (with a neighbor) while I went into camp for payment.

First I visited the school, made my bow to the Agent and staff and then chatted and giggled a while with Mrs. Dunn, the Superintendent.

My! my! my! How often during these long

years of "hard labor" have this splendid woman and her husband taken me in, hungry, dirty, muddy, half drowned and looking like a tramp to brush me, and shake me, and soothe me, and feed me, and laugh with me, and then push me into a nice clean room where there was always a roaring fire, a big pail of soft water, soap, and a bed covered with plenty of good warm "I D" blankets. Never, never, never shall I forget their kindness !

February 9th. Returning from the afternoon meeting in the pelting rain I tied up my tent early, lit the oil-stove and attacked the Christmas letters. I had not written half an hour before the tent began to flap vigorously, water sifted in from above and poured in under the canvas. Stacking things up as well as I could I waddled to the cot on my heels, spread the raincoat over it and took off shoes and skirt and stowed them under the pillows. Then I donned a thick flannel kimono, a hood, bedroom slippers and a pair of warm wristlets. Turning back the bedding I got in, wound my skirts well down about me, wrapped my feet in a shawl, tucked everything up out of the water, laid down, pulled the quilts up over my head, adjusted my Conversation tube so I could pipe in air, wiggled a little, and then said to myself : " Now let the wild world wag as it will. I'll be gay and happy still." Forgot my prayers, ironed the damp sheet with my cast-iron constitution and slept like a log.

February 10th. Before I was up Indian faces peeped in to see how I had weathered the storm. The rain, striking the long hump in the bed caused by the anatomy of the missionary, had splashed to the ground on both sides, and I lay in state, the proud possessor of an island home.

It rained all day and seated on the cot with my feet on the dish-pan, turned bottom side up, I wrote fifteen letters, my head covered with one layer of raincoat and my back and bed with the other. The dogs were a botheration. No sooner would I clear the tent and get back to my exalted position than long rows of noses and paws would begin to appear under the canvas. Finally I struck on a plan that worked like a charm. Making a pile beside me, on the cot, of various articles I wrote on till a quarter of a dog was in the tent. Sometimes it was a frying-pan that struck it, sometimes a pot cover, a butcher knife, scissors, a can opener, quilt pegs, a whisk, soap, *The Standard, The Canadian Baptist, The Saturday Evening Post, Tidings,* etc. It made no difference what was sent after him, the result was always the same ; a shrill bark, a quick turn, a scramble and a swish of the vanishing point.

About five o'clock I bundled up and waded over to see Abe-ham. The father signed, " I

just do one thing. I sit all day and pray for
Abe-ham. To-morrow I will give you his last
Jesus money."

It was dark when I returned, too wet for a
meeting and too cold to write so I went to bed
immediately after supper. It was so cold the
water froze the cot to the ground. There was
nothing to do but shiver and shake till morning.

There are people who would have gotten up
and knelt in prayer but I wanted to fight to keep
up circulation. It is " Believe on the Lord Jesus
Christ " that saves, and *giving the Gospel to
every creature* that proves the sincerity of the
belief. Then why should I feel condemned because I didn't want to pray with the cold chills
running up and down my spine?

February 11th. Late in the afternoon Gahbein
appeared and with bowed head and trembling
hand prayed and handed in Abe-ham's last Jesus
money (five dollars for Baby Band and five dollars for the church). All hope was abandoned.

February 12th. A dog darted out of my tent
almost throwing me on my back as I came in
after the evening meeting. I chased him from
under every wagon, hack and buggy but with
none effect. The cot was wet and sloppy—dog-
on-it ! It was so cold, I got up and put rolls of
batting down my back in the middle of the night.
There was a goose to pick in the morning.

February 14th. Snow, wind, sleet and frost. In North Dakota it would be called a blizzard.

Don't talk to me about "a strenuous life." I don't call it strenuous to hunt lions and bears on a dandy horse in jolly company, in good health, in good clothes and in good spirits. And I don't call it strenuous to chop wood and carry water when you have both handy and *don't have to do either.* And I don't call it strenuous to do lots of other things when you are full of the best food in all lands with an occasional 'possom thrown in !

February 15th, Sunday. The camp-call rang out :

> "Come! come! hurry and come !
> The storm is bad.
> The wood is low.
> Everybody bring one stick.
> Come! come! hurry and come ! "

Wood arrived with every worshipper and as the ice melted on the top of the tent great sheets of water poured down upon the heads, backs and laps of the listeners. Nobody dodged or smiled. It is not the Indian's road to be surprised.

One testimony was interesting : "You all know me. Me and my wife get all stirred up sometimes. After it is over I try all I can. I take her on the neck and kiss her."

February 19th. Saddle Mountain at last ! Lucius unloaded the stuff in the yard and hurried on home. The Bear-woman beamed from the door. Seizing the tent poles I ran to the shed and fairly fired them up on their high shelf. Both bounded back. One struck me across the forehead and the other square on the nose. Clapping my handkerchief up to catch the blood I sat down to cry. There wasn't a drop. The Bear-woman took me on the neck and kissed me. There was a bag about that neck containing $166.81. ($131.15 of the amount was quilt-earned money and $144.98 of the total was for the church.)

Hurrah! Hurrah! Hurrah! The one thousend dollar mark for the building fund had been reached in the storm! Hurrah! Hurrah! Hurrah!

TOTAL RECEIPTS:

Indian contributions		$ 355.98
Missionaries		65.69
Unsolicited:		
" Rock Island Officials		200.00
" Dutch Reformed Indians ...		30.00
" Chinese, San Francisco and Oakland		12.50
" White friends		7.50
Curios sold		8.50
Pelts		8.20
Quilt money		311.63
Total		$1,000.00

Hurrah again!

IX

*The Opening Day—Organization and Dedication
—The First Lord's Supper—Minding their
own Business—Carrying the Gospel to the
Ghost-Dance Camp—Miss Bare's Departure
—The Divine Call—The Vote for a White
Pastor to Train Lucius—A Non-Voter—The
End*

APRIL 12, 1903. Seven years ago to-day
we held our first gospel service on Saddle
Mountain Creek with the rain pouring
down and "every creature" crowded into a
small two-room house. As Easter Sunday fell
upon the same date as the anniversary it was
unanimously decided that we celebrate both days
by the formal opening of the new church.

Owing to the tremendous strain of the winter's
work, the limited quarters and the near approach
of the organization and dedication, we did not
plan an elaborate service. No special invitations
were issued. There were no big guns from a
distance, no opening sermons and no closing
benedictions but the glory of the Lord filled the
place and His name was exalted among the
people.

As we were about to close the morning meet-

ing an Indian jumped up. "I know it 'tain't my
turn to talk," he said, " but I can't keep still any
longer for the tears is coming out on my skin all
over. Now you fellers—now—to-day—in this
new Jesus House we want you to give your
hearts to Him. You have been making fun of
us all these years, saying : ' The Saddle Mountain Kiowas are crazy for they can never build
a church.' We did not build it. We pushed
hard to send the Gospel to the Hopis and Jesus
pushed hard for us. He done it and He will do
more wonderful things for you in your heart to-
day if you open and let Him in. We are praying for a Kiowa young man to be our pastor
now and when He answers this, our hearts will
be full up."

Boton had passed away and it was Ah-mah-
hah, wife No. 2, who arose. Wrapping the
blanket more tightly about her she said with
quivering lips : "Many times the Holy Spirit
has spoken to my heart but I have held back.
They would not take me in when my husband
lived. . . . To-day when my little son stood
up in this new Jesus House and read from the
Book, the Holy Spirit touched me again and I
get up to tell you I have given my heart to Jesus
and am ready to be baptized as soon as I have
a chance."

Mrs. Dunn kindly postponed the Easter Exer-
cises at the Government School in order to let

the children in our district, about thirty in number, come home for the celebration. Many of them had been prayed for before they were born, and had given to send the Gospel to others, and to the building fund since before they could remember. Some were saved and some were unsaved.

In two long rows they stood dressed in their pretty school uniforms, and the parents were invited forward to bid them welcome. It was a thrilling moment. In the twinkling of an eye the whole congregation scrambled up off the floor and made a rush to the front. Parents clasped children, children clasped parents, praying and crying, laughing and singing. Aside from the rest with eyes filled with tears Gahbein stood. "Oh! Abe-ham, my son! my son!" he sobbed.

May. We, the undersigned, have inspected the work of the contractors and are more than satisfied with the way in which they have filled the contract in every particular.

AKOMETO. DOYBI. DAWTOBI.

As these Inspectors marched proudly to the front "to touch the pen" every heart accompanied them and when they turned to go back every face burst into smiles and pent-up feelings escaped in song.

We had planned for a simple building in order to send the Gospel to others. True, we had dreamed of artistic beauty but our ambitions only included a stone foundation, four walls, a floor, a ceiling, a chimney, two doors and windows of plain glass.

Living beauty cannot be transferred to canvas. Nature did not express all that was in the loving heart of God. A Living Sacrifice made mountains, hills and valleys speak. The Great Spirit, the Creator, saw the mission in Hopiland, knew the living burning sacrifice it represented and breathed upon the poor little plans for our church. Instead of four walls He gave us six, instead of plain ceilings He gave us panels, instead of cheap windows He gave us stained glass and instead of an empty belfry He gave us a bell and a clock. It was truly the beauty of the Lord that filled the place.

August 28–30, 1903. It was no fun getting ready for the great event. The contractors began work on the house the same day that they finished the church. As the den (taken over by the Society) was to be dining-room and kitchen for the new house, a door was cut through as soon as the framework of the new building was up. By securing extra help we got possession as the last sun sank. How we worked ! Shavings, lathes, sawdust, split nails and general debris were sent skiting out the up-stairs door, down over the veranda, and mops, sapolio, clean rags and water were handled vigorously.

A little door had been cut through up-stairs into the space above the den and in this we had been storing various supplies for weeks. As we had every single thing in readiness it did not take long to settle.

Cots were the main articles of furniture and we made them up with the whitest of sheets and pillow-cases and dainty pink comforts. Biscuit boxes covered neatly with white oilcloth served as wash-stands and smaller boxes covered with cretonne for seats. Humble furnishings, perhaps, but they brought *mahogany feelings* to us two girls. There was not the slightest danger of either of us threatening "to go home to-morrow," now.

Miss Bare was in her room making her toilet. Let me say that over again; in her room making her toilet. How civilized it sounds. I was arranging my beloved books in my room, before making my toilet. Think of it. Suddenly the door burst open and in bounded Mrs. Parker, Captain Parker, Miss Parker, Mr. Rowley and Dr. Williams, all from Chicago. Captain Parker, as Vice-President of the Rock Island Railroad, had brought the party to Mountain View in his private car and knowing that we would be crowded brought tents which were soon set up in the yard.

Dr. and Mrs. Murrow and Miss Burdette were the other guests from a distance. How sorry we were not to be able to entertain in the new house all the tired missionaries, but the thing was out of the question.

They were Rev. and Mrs. Clouse, the faithful, from the Kiowas at Rainy Mountain, Rev. and Mrs. Deyo, the plodders from the Comanches at Fort Sill and poor sick Mr. Hamilton and Miss Jayne from the Cheyennes and Arapahoes at Watonga. Rev. and Mrs. Hicks from Elk Creek were absent but not forgotten.

Escorting Miss Burdette to my bed I said: "During my employ by the Women's Baptist Home Mission Society you have had me in many a tight place. It affords me inexpressible pleasure at this time to be able in a measure to return the compliment. This is my famous box-bed. In it I sleep in the winter time and on it in the summer. During this celebration you are to sleep *in it* and if necessity arise I will shut down the cover and sleep on it as usual." How the laughter went up through the lathing! Miss Bare and I, though aching in every joint, were supremely happy.

It was interesting to watch the visitors all give little starts as they entered the church. " Well! well! well!" said Captain Parker, rubbing his hands and glancing all round from floor to ceiling. "Well! my! You certainly have built a pretty little church away out here."

"How much is it worth?" I ventured to ask.

"Twenty-five hundred at the very least." (The Indians paid one thousand and the Women's Baptist Home Mission Society four hundred for the industrial rooms.)

Colonel Randlett marched to the middle of the building with military step, took in everything with one sweep of his quick eye and swallowing hard said: "Why! We haven't anything like this at Anadarko."

Mrs. Parker hugged us all up tight in her arms and said: "Why didn't you tell us you were going to be so grand?"

But Miss Burdette was the proudest of all. Every time I caught her eye during the eventful days that followed it seemed to say: "My dear Isabel, you have not been a model missionary. You have given us many a merry chase, but this church certainly is a model. It goes beyond my highest expectations."

Sunday was the big day. The Indians' much beloved and "long-time-ago-friend," Dr. J. S. Murrow, was naturally master of ceremonies.

The first two days had been given over to hearing testimonies from the sixty-four members who had been dismissed from Rainy Mountain to form the new church. Now the great ceremony was to take place. The interpreter responded to all questions. Poor Lucius! His heart hit him so hard he could hardly speak.

"Is it your desire to give this house to God?" asked Dr. Murrow. "Yes, yes, sir," came the answer, with the emphasis on the sir.

"Is there any debt on the building?" Debt? debt? debt? That sounded familiar. With perhaps one or two exceptions all were in debt and ever had been, but debt on the Jesus House? That was a different thing. "No sir!" came the answer triumphantly. A big Bible and the keys of the church were then handed over and that finished Lucius. He couldn't have said, "Yes sir," or "No sir" again without medical assistance.

Rev. H. H. Clouse gave the Articles of Faith, Rev. R. Hamilton, Church Covenant, Rev. C. E. Deyo, Words of Recognition, and Miss Burdette offered the dedicatory prayer. "God's-Light-upon-the-Mountain" Mission Circle had been purposely let die that, Phœnix-like, "God's-Light-upon-the-Mountain Baptist Church" might rise from its ashes. Miss Bare was chosen clerk and treasurer and the following nominated as deacons: Gahbein, Akometo, Tonemoh and Spotted Horse.

"I trust you have prayed earnestly," said Dr. Murrow, "and selected men full of the love of Jesus. Are you ready to vote?"

With a face as sober as a judge Odlepaugh arose and said : "I am first motion." "And I am second motion," said Mon-cha-cha, with equal gravity.

Six candidates were received for baptism and then all scattered for dinner, "crazy with happy" as the Indians expressed it.

The afternoon service was given over to the visitors, Dr. Murrow presiding.

Commissioner Leupp had been expected but at the last minute hastened on to Washington, sending a contribution to the plate (which was put in the pew fund).

Colonel Randlett was introduced first. "This is not the agent's day," he said. "It is the preacher's day. This is not a council room, but the House of God. I am sorry I am not a preacher instead of an agent. I would rather be an honest, sincere preacher who has led a single one of you on the Jesus road to stay, than to have all the glory that has come to me as a soldier or an Indian agent. You may lose your faith in agents and maybe in preachers but have faith in God. I am glad your missionaries have taught you that it is a part of religion to work. I have seen Indians of many tribes but I never saw any who built for themselves such a church as this. I may not be with you again but I hope some day to meet you in the Beautiful Home where we shall know one another better than we have here. I shall certainly remember this day to the close of my life."

Captain Parker, carrying a splendid big "Stars and Stripes," came handsomely forward next. "I suggest," he said, "that when Colonel Randlett ceases to be your agent you secure him as your pastor. I am glad to be here to-day. Some years ago I saw this magnificent valley and mountain for the first time but I did not know much about the people. Later I heard that you wanted to build a church and I was privileged to help a little. To-day I have seen its dedication. You have worked hard but you will be better for it. I have brought to your church the flag of our country and yours. Washington wishes its Indian children well. Law rules the universe. By obeying the laws of the Great Spirit you become strong in body and strong in soul and best honor your flag, your country and your God. When you see this flag think on these things."

It was Miss Burdette's turn next. Eee! but she was happy and her heart hit her hard too.

"My heart is big with joy to-day," she said. "Jesus has been my Leader for nearly fifty years and I stand here to tell you He has been a Good Leader. Your church is beautiful! beautiful! beautiful!" Then she told how she had been interested in the Indians since before the Jesus Women's Society was organized when her Sunday-school class sent Dr. Murrow twelve dollars to help with the work.

At the close of her talk she, Dr. Murrow, Captain Parker, and Colonel Randlett were all led to the front by Indian escorts. Popebah presented Miss Burdette with five dollars for the new Training School. Sape-mah presented Dr. Murrow with five dollars for his Indian Orphanage. Mabel presented Captain Parker with five dollars for his new church in Chicago and Akometo presented the agent with bow and arrows to add to his splendid Indian collection.

Of course there were responses and then away we all went like the breeze to a natural baptistry in the foot-hills of the mountains where the six happy converts were buried beneath the wave.

Dr. Williams preached in the evening, the deacons were ordained, the right hand of fellowship was extended to "the first borned" and then with singing, crying, laughing, praying and hand-shaking the celebration closed.

An Indian woman summed up the feelings of the whole Kiowa settlement in these words: "When I seen our Jesus House going up with my two eyes my heart began to grow and as the church got bigger my heart got bigger and bigger and bigger. To-day it is all busted to pieces."

CHARTER MEMBERS

1. Lucius Aitsan
2. Mabel Aitsan
3. Amos Aitsan
4. Minnie Aitsan
5. Jessie Aitsan
6. Akometo
7. Doymah Akometo
8. Tonacho
9. Odlepaugh, son of Santanta
10. Ananthy Odlepaugh
11. Spotted Horse
12. Hattie Spotted Horse
13. Kokom
14. Popebah Kokom
15. Tonemoh
16. Tone-gah-gah
17. Keapetate -Tone - gah - gah
18. Papedone
19. Sapemah Papedone
20. Dawtobi
21. Gee - ah - ga - h o o d l e Dawtobi
22. Mon-cha-cha
23. Mrs. Mon-cha-cha
24. Ate-umbah Domot
25. Mahyan
26. Longhorn
27. Ba-ah-tate-Longhorn
28. Gahbein
29. Heenkey
30. Satezadlebe
31. Hoke-do-dah
32. Queototi
33. Agoptah
34. Addletape Satezadlebe
35. Guonemah
36. Agomah
37. Stella
38. Ruth Odlepaugh
39. Bettie Odlepaugh
40. Fanny Kokom
41. Bessie Kokom
42. Wesley Kokom
43. George A-he-ah
44. Herman Bahlah
45. Mrs. H. Bahlah
46. Julia Hunt
47. Taryule
48. George Hunt
49. Blanche Kokom
50. Mrs. Tonemoh
51. Robert Onko
52. Felix Thompson
53. Dick Boton
54. Mrs. Queototi
55. Mrs. Apole
56. Mina Domot
57. Whitefeather
58. Chaino
59. Mrs. Chaino
60. Eddie Longhorn
61. Ah-to-mah
62. Captain Hall
63. Mrs. Hall
64. Isabel Crawford

Julia, Ahtomah, Mahyan and Sapemah were members of the church before the work began at Saddle Mountain, and with very few exceptions all had heard the Gospel before from faithful missionaries of various denominations, especially Revs. Methvin (Methodist), Fait (Presbyterian), Carithers (Cumberland Presbyterian), Hicks and Clouse.

September 12th. The Indians had asked repeatedly: "When we build our Jesus House may we have the 'Jesus Eat' (the Lord's Supper) and mind our own business?"

To-day the Ordinance was explained carefully. "It is a simple service, so simple that any church can observe it whether it is rich or poor, large or small. It is a *Church Ordinance* and should not be carried into associations, conventions or any other place. It belongs to the Church and the Church only. Jesus wanted to give His children some simple things to do in remembrance of Him. His Gospel was simple, most of His talks were simple, His life was simple, the Holy Spirit's work was simple and everything Jesus did was plain and simple and full of heart.

After He had eaten His last supper with His disciples He just leaned over, picked up a piece of bread and breaking it said: 'This is my body broken for you; eat it and remember me.' They did not understand but they did what He told them. Then He poured out a cup of red grape juice saying: 'This is my blood shed for you.' They did not understand yet but they drank it and wondered. He only said: 'Do this often for my sake,' and after singing a hymn they all went out.

Not till after Jesus was crucified did they understand what it meant and then they remembered. Ever since, all over the world, big churches and little churches, with pastors and without pastors, observe this simple ordinance, not because the members love one another so much but because they *love Jesus more* and want to obey His exact commands."

Lucius was the unanimous choice of the church as administrator. (They voted on it first Indian way, and then white way without a dissenting voice.)

September 27th. The account of the first Lord's Supper was read. Lucius and the deacons took their places. Prayers were offered. The elements were handed by Lucius to the deacons and from the deacons to the people, including the missionaries.

A thank offering of $10.25 was given. They sang an hymn and went out.

It was Gahbein who spoke : "All you young men look at me. I am half blind but when I passed the bread and wine I was not ashamed, for I remembered Jesus. I have a son, a little son and I love him very much. He is with Jesus now but when I look at his picture on my coat I remember him. It is kind of Jesus to ask us to look at the bread and wine and remember Him the same way.   Oh Abe-ham ! my son, my son ! "

December 24th, Saturday.   Christmas, 1903, was one never to be forgotten.   When the giv. ing-to-Jesus time came the congregation went wild.   They rushed to the table in crowds and the money tumbled into the four baskets at such a rate that no correct accounts could be kept. There were $102.70 in cash, and $100 in pledges for a church at Hog Creek.   It was touching to see fathers with little children in their arms, mothers with babies in theirs and other children clinging to both, giving money by families into the treasury of the Lord.   One woman elbowed her way to the table holding a handkerchief by one corner with money knotted in the other three.   Some of the members who could not be present sent money from ten to fifty miles.

A china pig was brought in with this letter : I want you to know that I send this pig with some money in it for Baby Band for my little son Judson.   I remember the very night the Lord gave him to me.   It was August 10th, in the morning before day came.   The first thing I thought of was this, when my mother told me he was a boy : " Oh, Father in Heaven ! I am so thankful that Thou hast been watching over me and my son.   And now wilt Thou be with me while I raise him. Teach me how to keep him well." I am sorry I cannot be with you. Be sure and pray for my little son Judson.

BLANCHE KOKOM.

A beautiful silver communion service, the gift of our kindly agent, was cause for special enthusiasm but " Thank you, Jesus ! Thank you; Jesus ! Thank you, Jesus ! You have been kind to us and saved six of our poor lost souls !" were the way-ahead signs made, as one after another blanketed form passed out into the starlight after the first Christmas tree in the completed church.

On Christmas (Sunday) morning the happy converts were examined after making their talks.

Botallee : " Before I was converted I came twice to this church. I was so surprised, for I heard something very new. Before I came I never hunted for Jesus anywhere. Now I believe Jesus has changed my heart and the Holy Spirit has made me come forth."

Chaino (in tears) : " He is my brother. I have been praying for him very earnestly and now I am so glad I don't know what to do. I try to take care of myself in the bad places and you must do the same."

Questions :

" Botallee, do you believe you are truly converted ? Has the Holy Spirit shown you the way and not yourself ? If you take the Jesus road are

you going to let the old roads go? Are you
willing to work for Jesus and for yourself?"

Answer:

"There is just one bad thing I like. Cards.
Since I began to get ready to follow Jesus I never
go near where they are. I believe Jesus will
help me to cut off this bad road. I believe I am
truly converted, for Jesus has saved me."

Onko: "I am a very quiet man. When I
heard the Gospel I was so anxious to be saved
that I went to all the camp-meetings hunting for
Jesus. I heard that 'the little water-road' was
not true so I stood, stopped and prayed very
earnestly to the Great Father to show me the
way. The Holy Spirit has brought me here. I
believe 'the big water-road' is right."

Question:

"My cousin, I know your heart and I am much
pleased with you. Are you willing to work for
Jesus and help with the work over here; and are
you going to plow more?"

Answer: "Yes."

Nancy: "My heart is my own. Nobody can
boss it but myself. I have given it to Jesus. It
is full of 'happy' because I have started on the
Jesus road."

Question:

"You live a long way off, where no churches
are. It will be hard for you to stand fast. Are
you going to teach your children right?"

Answer: "Yes I am."

Sophie Akometo: "Because both my parents are Christians I ——" overcome with tears.

Questions:

"Are you sure you really love Jesus in your heart? Do you want to be baptized to please Him and not your parents? Does the Holy Spirit make you know you are saved?"

Answer: "Yes."

Saudle: "I give myself to Jesus with all my heart and I believe He has forgiven me all my sins. My husband has been praying for me so long. I am glad I have found the way."

Question:

"If you are really converted are you going to cut off the cards and the dance?"

Answer: "Yes."

Domdadle: "I was just like sick for Jesus last night. I did not look for Him right before. He is the only One who can save me. I have given Him my heart and I believe He has saved me and forgiven my sins. I am only a woman but I will lead my children right."

Long Horn made the talk to the converts: "When a man has a chill he shakes. I am so happy to-day because so many have been saved that I shake for joy all over. I am an old man and I know all about the old Indian religions. There is no power in any of them. Jesus' road has the power. Your souls are saved now and when you finish this life your body will drop off and be put into the grave but your souls will go up to Jesus. He will put new flesh and new skins on them and then you will never die."

Heenkey arose: " Who will baptize these people? We have had the ' Jesus Eat,' but there is no one to do the baptizing. We ought to have an Indian pastor. Once I raced on the Fourth of July. They did not think my horse was very good but it came out ahead and the people clapped their hands and hollered. The missionaries have trained us and we are going faster and faster. Lucius is in the lead. We want him to be our pastor that our hearts may laugh."

The candidates were baptized as usual at Rainy Mountain by Pastor Clouse. After the Christmas rush was over I sent for the interpreter and said: " Now, Lucius, listen. We must take time for a little talk. You know your people are constantly asking if you can be their pastor and I want to explain everything very carefully to you again.

The church is a *spiritual* organization. God's plan is that the pastors shall be *spiritual* leaders, and all the members *spiritual* also, because the work to be done can only be accomplished through *spiritual power.* Men can go to school and study to be *anything they choose*—doctors, lawyers, teachers, etc., anything *except ministers. God chooses the men for the ministry.* He called Samuel three times before he knew what it meant.

He called Paul just once, suddenly. Both men *knew in their hearts* that they were called. *If God wants you He will call you. The voice of your people is not the voice of God.* Now let us pray."

Thoughtfully the reply came later: "I have prayed a whole lot about it since I understood about the spiritual call business. I told Jesus I was willing if He wanted me, but I would not put myself in. He has said nothing back to my heart yet. I think myself I can do better work for Him interpreting. Every time you talk I ask Jesus to just let me say what He tells you and not put in no words of my own. I think this is what Jesus wants me to do, but I will keep looking to Him for orders right along. I have spoken."

February 27, 1904. A committee had been appointed at Christmas time to visit three "straying members" and to-day it reported. Spotted Horse said: "I invited my cousin to eat dinner with me to make her heart glad first and then I said to her: 'You are a Christian. You have joined the Ghost-Dance. The Christians are all sorry and have sent me to ask you what is in your heart and bring them back words.'

She replied: 'It it true. I used to go to church and I wanted my eldest son to pick up the Jesus road and I talked to him about it. He loves mescal and the missionaries kick it, so he joined the Ghost-Dance and took the feather and I joined with him. Jesus is coming July 15th at twelve o'clock.'

I said: 'Are you going to throw away the Jesus road and stay with the Ghost-Dance? Do you want time to think about it? You know if Christians pick up another road we scratch out their names. Shall we wait for you?'

She did not answer but put down her head."

Gahbein gave in his report next. "You 'pointed me to see my aunt. I was sorry to do it but I went for Jesus' sake. I said to her this: 'You have walked on the Jesus road for a long time and now you have walked off it with your feet (danced). Why have you done it? Think about it and tell me so I can tell the others.' She said back to me this: 'You are like my own son and I am always sorry for you. You got no children. They come and go. I know you trust in Jesus with all your heart then why won't He let you keep your children? He loves you not. That is why I joined the dance road.' It was like fire in my heart and I said: 'Are you going to stay on that bad road and do you want your name cut off? Answer me that.' She said: 'Cut my name off. I am going to stay with it.'"

The other weak one said: "I have no bad feelings against the church. My brother led me off and I have missed the Jesus road. I must follow on now and if my brother goes to hell I must go with him. I know the missionaries love me but I can't help it. Jesus is coming July 15th at twelve o'clock."

The joint committee made the following recommendation: "We have talked it all over very carefully. Jesus wants us to keep clean His spiritual church and we have to do it. Two have cut themselves off but one did not answer and put down her head. We think we should wait for her till she answers after July 15th at twelve o'clock."

The report was accepted and acted upon and then poor sick Domdadle arose and said: "I was glad to hear the Gospel to-day. I am sick but Jesus is a wonderful helper. I have a little money I don't want to keep back from Him." Advancing to the table she took the cover off her Jesus-money-barrel and taking out of it a piece of purple velvet produced from its folds two cents and said: "This is the first money I saved for Jesus after I was converted." Then in order came a five-cent piece, a ten, a quarter, another quarter and a fifty-cent piece, in all $1.17. "Jesus has helped me right along and my Jesus money has grown bigger and bigger day by day. I am a happy woman giving it all to Him to-day, for He has done so much for me. I want all my brothers and sisters to pray for me."

"I want to tell you Christians something,"

said Pie-gad. "All the tribe calls me a very wicked man and I know it. The Christians are against me but the great Father and Jesus want to save me. I belonged to the Rainy Mountain Church and tried hard, but they cut me off and then I got mad and tried to hurt them. The Holy Spirit told me a great many times to stop it but the devil held me fast. I want to start again on the Jesus road and join this church if the Christians will help me."

I replied, "We are all glad you feel that you have sinned, for you have. That is true. Jesus and your brothers and sisters will forgive if you ask them and show that you are sorry. If I should steal something from Lucius I would not go to Kokom and ask him to forgive me. You must go back to the Rainy Mountain Church and ask for forgiveness. If it takes you back and you walk straight for a while it will give you a letter to join with us. Then you must come back to your farm and go to work."

Lucius: "Miss Crawford, he is a very wicked man and very weak but we all want to help him. We better 'point two strong Christians to go with him to help him through for he may not go alone."

The committee was appointed but the repentance was not unto good works.

March 12, 1905, Sunday. "We have had an

awful fire," said Lucius. "It came over the hills so fast that we had to burn out to meet it to save the church. It made me think of the judgment and I was sorry for those not saved.

Some of you have brothers and sisters lost and you ought to try hard to get them back from the fire. We ought to go to the Ghost-Dance camp regularly for if they are not saved when Jesus comes they will be all burned up.

Let us work together strong, not lazy on the Jesus road; let us be lively teams; let us be good workers. There is no other Friend like Jesus and no other Saviour."

Odlepaugh, Ananthy, Spotted Horse, Hattie and myself were appointed to go to the Ghost-Dance camp the next Sunday although this objection was raised: "The men are all right but the devil will beat the women and make them talk about something else."

March 20th. The Indian men, with Tonemoh added, went. All the women but myself stayed at home. With eyes and mouths firmly set and limbs somewhat trembley they entered the crowded medicine tepee. The meeting was in session but Indian courtesy turned it over to us. I said a few kind things, talked a while about " The altar to an unknown God," and then called upon Lucius. He was nervous but decided and among other things said: " If you could make my two eyes see Jesus in this tepee and you said to Him : 'This is Lucius, Jesus,' I would not believe it. I would say : 'Jesus, you told us in your Book what to believe and I believe it and I won't believe anything else.' "

Odlepaugh spoke with heaving breast : "Amon, you and I were boys together. We parted when I picked up the Jesus road. You know me very well. I had a very bad temper and hurried up to get mad always. You see I am getting over it. I go to the Jesus House and listen, and listen, and listen, and I try, and try, and try and it is Jesus and His Holy Spirit who are helping me.

We have not come over here to talk about ourselves but to bring you God's message. We are hungry to have you give your hearts to Jesus."

Tonemoh was the coolest of all. He said : "You all know me also. I used to eat mescal every time I got a chance. You don't see me there any more. I keep going, going, going to the Jesus House, getting spiritual food from the Book and now the devil does not temptation me. We have come here to-day to try and help you find the Jesus road."

Poor Spotted Horse was almost overwhelmed but after a terrible struggle managed to speak. "You all know what a 'shamed (bashful) man I am. I'm 'shamed about everything. When I was growing up I was so 'shamed I hided myself and never went where the crowds were. After I gave my heart to Jesus I was changed altogether but it is hard for me to talk yet.

In my heart I am not 'shamed of Jesus. He has done wonderful things for me and I love Him very much. I am not ashamed to stand before Jesus and tell you I'm saved. I want you to open your hearts to Him and let the Holy Spirit show you the way to be saved. You all know my father and mother stand with you on the Ghost-Dance road. I have talked to them a little about finding Jesus but I was so 'shamed it was hard. After to-day I won't be so 'shamed and I will talk to them plainly Jesus has saved me and that is why I am not 'shamed to come here to-day and ask you to look for Jesus. If I do not shake hands and laugh and talk with you you must not mind. In my heart I shake hands with you and want you to be saved."

Amon thanked us for the visit, invited us to come again and said they were all ready to be saved as soon as the Holy Spirit showed them the way.

One by one we filed out of the tepee. Silently we got into our carriages and with faces turned to the Jesus House followed the new roads back to our homes.

Going into all the world and preaching the Gospel to every creature is a very different thing from giving it to your relations and friends at home.

September 1st.   Miss Bare " is going home to-morrow " all right, to be married to a man named *Cooper!*   It is a piece of black hand work.   (See page 162.)   What shall I do without her?

ASSOCIATIONAL REPORT, 1905

Gospel meetings, 101.   Missionary and industrial meetings, 43.   Funerals, 6.   Letters written, 914.   Miles travelled (not railroad), 687. Money raised, $549.95 (including $270 quilt money).   Received by baptism, 25.   By experience, 2.   By letter, 1.   *Total membership, 100.* Lord's Supper administered by pastors, 7.   By Lucius, 2.   Omitted, 3.

December.   The agent has written congratulating our Indians on having the best crops this year of all the tribes of the agency.   The government reports are all in.   Hurrah!

June 12, 1906.   The Association met at Saddle Mountain.   How proud we were of the church, the dining hall (costing $1,003.79—over $700 of the amount quilt money), the beautiful baptistry, Mrs. Topping (the house mother), the windmill and our $724.79 Jesus money for the year!   Miss Burdette and Mrs. Donnalley from " away back

East " and Miss McLean and her two Hopis (our spiritual papooses) were the special guests.

It was fitting that little Sarah Aitsan, who gave the first dime and dollar to the building fund, should be among the forty-nine candidates baptized in the new baptistry.

But another event of great importance took place.

In response to a special call the church assembled and Lucius made the following statement :

" Ever since this church was organized many of you have wanted me to be the pastor. I've only been to school four years so I told you that I did not want you to push me in. I knew that Jesus would talk to my heart if He wanted me to do this work and that is why I held myself back. I wanted to hear His voice first and I kept thinking—thinking—thinking and praying a whole lot. It was at Watonga I heard the whisper first. I had been thinking very carefully and I thought this : ' If I am pastor all the boys who went to school and are smart will laugh at me and the Ghost-Dance people too.' But my heart said : ' Never mind if they do ; you will be a great help to your people.' When I felt this I said : ' No use for me to be afraid to work for Jesus and my people.' Then Jesus spoke to my heart and this is what He said : ' Lucius, you have worked for Me many years and picked up My words right along. I want you to do this work for Me.' When I heard this my heart just like shook. It moved and hit very fast and then I knew that God had called me. Look at me. How poor I am to serve the Lord. I am not fit to be the pastor of this church but if Jesus wants me to be I'm willing. I have spoken."

The deacons responded and with one consent all began to say : "We have had another great blessing from the Lord."

> " After long agony
> Rapture of bliss
> Strange was the pathway
> Leading to this."

DEAR MISS BURDETTE :

On Sunday, August 19, 1906, thirty-one of the thirty-four members present of the Saddle Mountain Church voted to ask for a pastor for one year to teach Lucius. We write to inform you of the fact and to ask that you attend to the correspondence relative to the matter.

Written on behalf of the church,
ISABEL CRAWFORD.

P. S. I beg leave to state that the coming of a pastor to Saddle Mountain will be in accordance with my most earnest endeavor for nine long years. I have worked for it, talked for it and prayed for it and at last when the end seems almost in sight I find my heart straining itself to keep back the glad shout of victory. Not

because it is my way but because it is His way
that a New Testament Church should have as
its head a *man called of God and* set apart by
his brethren to perform the duties of pastor.

I. C.

August 25th. Odlepaugh called. After sitting in a *brown* study for a long time he finally
signed: "When anybody else gets mad I always get madder. I did not vote. I drove to
Elk Creek (forty miles) and went to church there.
I have come here to-day to make a talk to you.
A long time ago when the white people took my
father to jail he got mad, jumped out the window and was killed. It is the Indian road when
anybody is captured or killed like that for the
nearest relative to go on the war-path and get a
scalp. Big George's brother, Comahty, Kiowa-
Bill, Honeyme-a-daw, White Buffalo, Apole,
Paudlekeah, Papedone and others now dead
went with me a long way off, to where the white
people lived. We hid along the river till we saw
three men coming and then we sprang out and
our arrows killed two. The other got away.
We scalped the two we killed and left their
bodies in the middle of the road to skeer other
white people coming along. When we got home
we put the scalps on a long pole and danced
round it. My heart was happy then for I had
got even about my father.

Another time we went off on the war-path. I

was about twenty. We hid along a river in Texas and soon a white man in a little buggy driving a mule came along. We jumped out at him and took off his hair. He had a leather bag and we cut it all to pieces with our knives and scattered the letters everywhere. We did not know what money was then and some of the young men brought the bills home with them and rolled them into cigarettes and smoked them.

Old Odlepaugh gathered a big ball of them and put them in his shield which was buried with him.

Another time Long Horn, Ahtape, Mon-cha-cha, Red Eagle and others now dead went on the war-path. They saw a wagon with four mules coming with two soldiers and the pay chief. They sprang out of the timber, killed and scalped the chief, tore up the money bags and got away. The two soldiers jumped into the river and swam across. We shot at them but did not hit them.

When the white Jesus man comes I will tell Him these dangerous stories and He will get 'skeered' and run and I will be glad. I want Him not. I stand with the Jesus women. I have spoken."

Chicago, 4026 Grand Boulevard.
MY DEAR MISS CRAWFORD :
It was such a disappointment that you could not have arrived yesterday in time for the Board meeting that we might have seen you and

assured you of our love and tenderest sympathy. It was my privilege to read to the members of our finance committee your wonderfully beautiful letter to the Saddle Mountain Church. I say yours—yet it seemed more like the Master's message to His loved ones and surely His spirit dictated that letter.

We, ourselves, could not keep the tears back and our hearts go out with a great loving tenderness to you and the band of noble Christians at Saddle Mountain.

I cannot but hope that in time Lucius will be the ordained pastor and you will be back to help guide and instruct as in all these faithful years past. We are praying that God will guide and make known His will in this matter and that He will tenderly care for His Indian children until His will is accomplished.

That He will sweetly rest and comfort you as He alone can—and through it all know you have our love.

With tenderest love,

(Mrs. John) IDA S. NUVEEN.

December 5, 1906.